'The church today tends to be other than Jesus. Yet, the Father is arranging a scenario at the end of the age which will clearly demonstrate the glory of his Son over every opposing passion.

'Paul White does an excellent job in this gripping biblical account of knowing Jesus through the power of the Holy Spirit, with a foundation of the Father's love. In Paul, I've observed a man after the heart of God who leads with an anointed youthfulness, attracting many to the One who captures his heart. His pioneering published work in *The Christing* is sure to be a hit as it draws the reader into deep truths through fascinating stories and truths from the Word all woven with an unusual writing style. This work will awaken the heart to the beauty of Jesus.'

Revd Patricia Bootsma
Associate Leader, Catch the Fire Ministries, North, South and
Central America;
itinerant speaker and author

'I have known Paul for many years. I count him as a true man of God, a wonderful friend and brother in Christ. What you have here is a rendition of Paul's heart – a heart shaped by Jesus to bring insight and creative warmth into our own Christian journey. When I read what is written it's as if Paul is in the room with me – I hear his voice and dwell in the wealth of his creativity, experience and wisdom. This is a book to sit with, mull over and ponder, like a multi-faceted jewel that you roll around your fingers in order to see the different light. Take it slowly and let God warm your heart with deep truth.'

Revd Canon Tony Stephens (retired)
formerly of The Callington Cluster, Diocese of Truro

'When you spend time with Paul, you know you're spending time with someone who has spent time with Jesus. He carries such a life, a passion, an energy, an enthusiasm that is contagious. My hope and prayer for you is that this excellent book increases your desire to spend time with King Jesus, living for him and carrying his presence to the world around you.'

Pete Baker
National Director, Pais Movement UK

'Paul White is the real deal. He is a man of God's Spirit who is firmly rooted in God's Word, and a deep thinker who is also a deep listener to the Lord. You will be challenged as you read this book to be the same. I encourage you to read it!'

Phil Moore
Lead Pastor of Everyday Church, London

'I have always been fascinated with the anointing. It is mind-blowing to me that God chooses to involve us, ordinary people, in unfolding his plans on the earth. In *The Christing*, author Paul White approaches the Bible with passion, clarity, simplicity and storytelling that is sure to engage everyone. I love Paul's ability to take the most outrageous concepts in the Bible and make them totally accessible. Don't hesitate, dive into this book and, in the process, you will be inspired to dive into the fullness of what God could and wants to do through you.'

Benjamin Jackson
Executive Director, Catch the Fire

The Christing

Mining the Bible to reveal the extravagant anointing of the Holy Spirit

Paul White

Authentic

27 26 25 24 23 22 21   7 6 5 4 3 2 1

First published 2021 by Authentic Media Limited,
PO Box 6326, Bletchley, Milton Keynes, MK1 9GG.
authenticmedia.co.uk

British Library Cataloguing in Publication Data
A catalogue record for this book is available from the British Library.

ISBN: 978-1-78893-173-1
978-1-78893-174-8 (e-book)

Cover design and illustrations by Paul White
Printed and bound by CPI Group (UK) Ltd, Croydon, CR0 4YY.

Copyright acknowledgements

Contents

Preface

This book is about Jesus: he is my passion.

The best thing that I could hope for from writing anything, is that it might help one more person to fall a bit more in love with the most awesome person to ever set foot on our beautiful planet. I love the way Jesus dances through the pages of the Bible; seen fleetingly in shadows and types, then suddenly blazing in all his glory before slipping away, to appear again later. He similarly has danced with me throughout the course of my life so far. I am continuously tantalised by the sweet encounters of his presence, with the promise of more keeping me hungry. I am rich and satisfied by his relentless kindness to me, yet envious of those who describe levels of encounter with my lover which are, as yet, unfamiliar to me.

For as long as I can remember, I have held the deepest desire to see the church of Jesus looking beautiful and glorious; an authentic representation of her soon-to-be husband. There is nothing more lovely to behold than ordinary people moving in the flow of the Holy Spirit, demonstrating his love and power to each other and to the world. I will be delighted if this book inspires someone to invest their life in the great task of making his church ready for him. I believe the world today is hanging by a thread, desperate to see the real deal lived out by ordinary Christians. I see the Western church torn by a major identity crisis, battling with ideology, cynicism and fear of public disapproval. Meanwhile, the people around us would love Jesus if only they could meet him: I believe it is our job to make sure they do.

To me, it is the most delightful paradox that the perfect, infinite God should limit himself in the performing of his ministry on earth by his unflinching determination to use frail human beings to represent him. I am always amazed at his patience; undone by his pursuit of my heart. I cannot claim any great credentials for writing this book, except that he loves me. This book is not an attempt at an academic work; it is the description of a still-unfolding journey of discovery, written for fellow explorers searching out the mysteries of God.[1]

Foreword

By Pastor Clive Jackson

Paul has been a dear friend for many years and he is one of the most authentic lovers of Jesus that I know. From his early days he has been a serious student of the Bible, always searching it to know the author rather than just gain academic knowledge. This book is packed with revelation of our heavenly Father's heart and is a delight to read. Paul traces the golden thread of the anointing and its practical relevance to all of us, as we become part of his-story. I love the way Paul gives the text a contemporary feel and how he sees the Bible through a clear understanding of the heart of the Father; it's both refreshing and helpful.

To Anna, you are truly a gift from God.

To Dave Scragg, a dear friend and
soldier of the cross.
1951–2020

My Introduction

the legendary Mini

As I reversed my parents' legendary Mini Clubman Estate (the first version) out of the yard, I had a feeling I recognised from childhood – that inexplicable joyful excitement in the belly; the feeling that it's your birthday, or that something good is going to happen today. It was a Sunday. I was home for the Christmas holiday from my first term at art college and was driving my two sisters to a church (new to us) about eight miles away. We had already attended the service there that morning. Everything about this church was different from what I was used to. Firstly, they were meeting in a school gymnasium rather than a chapel, then the age group – there were *young* couples with small children, then people sang the songs with their eyes shut and their hands in the air, and shockingly, people spoke out loud in tongues . . .

I had grown up in a tiny village in North Dorset in a devout household, with two parents who were serious about living the Christian life. At around the age of four, I told my dad I wanted a brother and he said that I should pray – I had two sisters and felt outnumbered. Some time later, Mum gave birth to my first brother, followed, three years after that, by a second. I knew then, from an early age, that God loved me and was interested in my prayers. In our family, Sundays involved getting dressed in our best clothes and staying clean for the whole day – tricky, as we kids were country hillbillies who were constantly playing outside and getting covered in mud. Our mum used to lament that she did not have nice clean children like other people (meaning one aunt in particular whose kids were perfect). Often, on the way to church, Mum would look back at her disappointingly grubby offspring over her shoulder, from the front passenger seat of the car, and go for the dreaded handkerchief. Then she would spit on it and grind away some offending marks on our not-so-cherubic faces.

Church itself was mostly dark-stained wood and sitting still. (More on that later.)

My older sister had left home for teacher training college in the north of England. During her first summer holiday she had been invited to a Bible week in Yorkshire. When she returned home, she was noticeably different. She was kind of nicer, and seemed more happy. She had always been the spiritual leader for us kids, but now she seemed to have shot forwards, like she had had some kind of power-up, and was now in another dimension. I was a little sour about it, as I thought I should be on the same level as her – I was reading the Bible and pray-ing every day, *and* going to the Gospel Hall mid-week Bible studies with my dad, *and* staying awake, which surely merited some consideration. The thing which affected me most of all, however, was a cassette tape of worship music, which my sis-ter played whilst she was in the bath. It was a recording made live at the Dales Bible Week the previous year. Something hap-pened on the inside of me when I heard that music which I had absolutely no grid for. It was as if my intestines were dis-integrating into a mush. I was mesmerised. At the end of some of the songs the singing continued but without distinguishable words. I now know that the people were singing in tongues, but then I had never heard anything like it. To me it sounded like music from another world.

From that moment on, my heart was enlisted on a quest to have whatever that feeling was and keep it. I knew what it would make me feel like, but I didn't know what *it* was. After that summer holiday, I left home myself and started at art college. I visited many churches in the town, always looking for that otherworldly feeling which the worship had evoked in me. To my great disappointment, I failed to find it anywhere, until I came home for the Christmas holiday. My sister announced to me that there was a really good church in Shaftesbury, a small market town not far from my parents' house. I was pretty sceptical as I hadn't heard of it. I was even more envious that my younger sister had been to visit my older sister and had been 'Baptised in the Holy Spirit'. So now she was in the club, and I wasn't. As I looked around this church, I could see that the people appeared to have something I did not. I thought, 'Either this is it, or they are pretty good at faking it!' The pastor was a dairy farmer, with rosy cheeks and fingers like sausages. When he preached, I was hooked. I could get what he was saying – it was not all remote and cerebral – I felt that I could actually do what he was talking about.

That evening I arrived at the service with the birthday sense of excitement. As I had been manoeuvring the car, an uninvited thought had invaded my mind: 'Tonight's your night.' As in the morning, the meeting began with worship. I knew one of the songs, but I knew I didn't know Jesus like these people did. Then they started singing, 'The greatest thing in all my life is knowing you . . .' I can feel it now, even as I write.

I was beginning to unravel inside. I wanted to really, really mean those words so badly, but I felt like a fraud. I began to weep. The floodgates burst open and I was sobbing beyond control. My sisters called the pastor over, who took me into a side room. I know that I was already a Christian – I had prayed the prayer to receive Jesus first when I was five years old. I already loved Jesus, but that night my world was transformed. The Holy Spirit filled me and I knew he had come.

The one thing my sisters, and others I had spoken to, cited as evidence of having been baptised in the Holy Spirit was the ability to 'speak in tongues'. This was scary but exciting territory, as the church culture I had experienced until then strenuously opposed speaking in tongues. These sincere believers clearly had no problem with the early disciples doing it, but assumed it must surely be the devil causing this phenomenon to resurface in the late 20th century. My secret fear prior to that evening, however, was that I would be prayed for to receive the Holy Spirit and it wouldn't work – I wouldn't feel anything at all, or be any different. Well, I really did feel it, and I really was very different afterwards. I felt as if someone had removed the top of my head and it was wide open to God with no obstruction in the way. I felt as though I was living under an open heaven, but I had never heard that expression before. My second fear was that I would not speak in tongues, and I didn't. The pastor, however, reassured me that I would definitely 'come through' in the next few days. I was a little disappointed that I hadn't burst out there and then. In fact, I had a sneaky suspicion that somehow my sin had made me too bad to get the full dose of the Holy Spirit. Thank God the Holy Spirit is a gift, not a merit award! In the end it took three weeks for me to start speaking in tongues – then, of course, I thought

I was making it up. I enjoyed it so much that I decided to keep 'making it up' a little longer! I have since spoken in tongues most days of my life.

From that point I knew that what had happened to me meant that all of the stuff I had read about in the Bible – the contents of the book of Acts, for example – was now possible. I knew that I had received the Holy Spirit and I could give my life to this.

All of my upbringing now made sense.

1: Open Heaven

Oily Rock

Jacob is running. Running for his life. His twin brother is big, red, hairy and angry. Angry with him. Jacob is the younger twin. When their mother gave birth to the boys, Jacob appeared still grasping his senior sibling's hairy heel. The pregnancy had been rough; an in-utero wrestling match with the two brothers fighting within the womb. At this point they are grown men, but things have not improved – Jacob is now running because his brother Esau wants to kill him. Esau is mad on two counts: firstly, Jacob tricked him out of his massive inheritance as the firstborn son; then, secondly, he deceived their father into giving him the unique blessing reserved for the oldest son. At this point in the narrative it's easy to sympathise with Esau – there is not much to like about his younger brother – Jacob appears to be living up to his name: *Grasper.*[1]

Night has fallen and Jacob is still running; fleeing to the home of his uncle, Laban. He stops to catch his breath, exhausted. Lying down, he rests his head on a rock and is overtaken by sleep. As he sleeps, he dreams. He is caught up in a dramatic spiritual moment: he watches as two worlds collide. He sees a stairway stretching up into heaven with angels going up and down, backwards and forwards from heaven to earth. Heaven is wide open before his very eyes. At the top of the stairway is

God himself. The God who called his father and grandfather is now speaking in person to Jacob, the fugitive – the cheat.

Open heaven

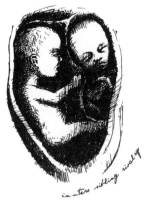

In this life-changing moment God renews promises he had made years before to his grandfather; now making them personally to Jacob. He promises to Jacob the very land he is lying on as a gift to him and his descendants. Jacob's response is profound. First, he makes a prophetic declaration: 'How awesome is this place! This is none other than the house of God, and this is the gateway of heaven' (Genesis 28:17). Second, he gives the area the name *Bethel*, meaning House of God. Third, he takes the stone he had laid his head on, hauls it up on its end, turning the pillow into a pillar. He is marking this place of encounter. God had just promised him that he would return to that spot – he is determined not to forget where it is. Fourth, he pours oil over the pillar – an anointed rock to mark the spot where heaven is opened to a man. Fifth, he vows to make God his God if he will provide for him and ultimately bring him safely home to his father's house. Sixth, he promises that the anointed stone will become God's house. Seventh, he promises a full tenth, or tithe, to God of everything material that God should ever give to him, such as sheep and goats.

This is a story turbocharged with layers of revelation. It is the first time the subject of anointing ever appears in the Bible.

Bible teachers have observed a principle which they call 'The Law of First Mention'. The idea is that when a subject is mentioned for the first time in the Bible, many elements which appear in the text at that time will consistently reappear throughout subsequent scriptural mentions of that subject. This story is the first biblical mention of a number of other important concepts including anointing, heaven opened and the House of God.

With no previous mention of anointing with oil in the Bible it is difficult as a 21st-century reader to comprehend what Jacob himself understood or meant to convey by his actions. Nowhere in the Bible, prior to this event, is it recorded that God would particularly like oil to be poured on a rock as a thing to please him. This appears to be an entirely spontaneous, voluntary action on Jacob's part. The Bible has many such expressions of worship which appear to be spontaneous and unprescribed, yet set precedents for future worshippers – we will take a look at some of them in the course of this book. Jacob clearly wanted to identify this place, where he had seen into heaven and where God had spoken to him, for the future.

There, but hidden

The glassy surface of the sea reflects the sky. If the sky is dark, the sea is grey and brooding; if the sky is blue, the sea looks like the pictures in a holiday brochure. The light of the sun flickers from the waves, but everything beneath is hidden. Take a scuba mask and dive below and you enter an entirely new world. The relatively flat surface of the sea is a membrane, approximately a single molecule thick, hiding billions of creatures, some no bigger than an individual cell, some far bigger than any land animal alive. Go deeper, and the mysteries are even more extreme. Scientists know more about the surface of the moon than they know about the silent depths of the sea. Crabs, shrimps and other fantastical animals and

plants don't just survive, but live their whole lives, feeding and reproducing in mineral-rich hot-water spouts in temperatures high enough to cook any normal organism. There are lonely deep-sea sharks equipped with massive eyes able to optimise the tiniest specks of phosphorescence in the utter blackness where no light from the sun can ever penetrate. Angler fish catch their lunch by dangling a bright light as bait from their own built-in fishing rod positioned in front of a grotesque collection of teeth. Below the skin of the sea is a kaleidoscope of bizarre fantasy creatures, some still waiting to be discovered.

Back into the womb

When a baby is conceived, this tiny speck of life embarks on a journey to the womb. There it proceeds to grow in an exclusive, purpose-built, temperature-controlled environment. The small person is surrounded by water strictly maintained at a steady 36°C, cushioned from shocks and bumps, and fed the perfect diet through a tube. All the oxygen required is supplied and all the waste products from the baby's body are hygienically disposed of by the mother's circulatory system. The outside world is out there, but very filtered. The yet unborn baby is remotely conscious of noises – they will become familiar with the tone of

Dad's voice as they grow (assuming he is still part of their life) even whilst in the womb. Other people, birds, cars – a billion things in this world surround them, but our baby is blissfully unaware. In order to begin to experience this world first-hand, they will have to be born.

Jesus once told a smart guy called Nicodemus that in order to see the kingdom of heaven, he would have to be 'born again'.[2] What an overused, misunderstood phrase that has become. In the 1980s, it was even used to market the new (now old) version of the Volkswagen Golf. However, Jesus was saying that Nicodemus would have to have a whole new beginning – to become alive spiritually – in order to see this world that was all around him, but hidden from him. He famously bantered with Jesus about getting back into his mother's womb, but was slightly missing the point. When Alice entered Wonderland she was unable to go through the tiny door into the beautiful garden until she drank from the bottle marked 'Drink Me'. Naturally speaking, we are far too big and important to get through the door to gain access to the kingdom of heaven. Jesus said, 'Unless you change [repent] and become like little children, you will never enter the kingdom of heaven' (Matthew 18:3 NIV, parenthesis added).

Heaven, or we could say the kingdom of heaven, is invisible to our natural eyes. It is the place, or dimension, that is home to God and his angels – glorious, otherworldly, spiritual beings who live to serve God. In heaven, the presence of God is unfiltered, the glory of God is the light that fills everything. No-one is sick, no-one is depressed, no-one is fighting. Heaven is always there, God is always worshipped and adored. On a normal day, human beings cannot see it. Yet it is, and always has been God's intention to live among mankind.[3]

Like the scuba mask, we need some means to enable us to see or enter this otherly dimension. At Bethel, Jacob was granted a backstage pass – a unique privileged access to glimpse what was to come much later through the Anointed One: heaven opened wide to all humanity, not just to one fugitive with a famous grandad. In this respect, Jacob was very much a prophet. He saw and named what was coming up in God's awesome eternal plan: Bethel, the House of God, the gateway to heaven. Surely that's what church is all about – a place where God lives among the people of the earth – a place where he can be easily found. Heaven opened means the resources, power and glory of the unseen heavenly realms made accessible; tangible and available to mortals.

David, the great prophetic worshipper, saw this too, and partially succeeded in bringing it about when he constructed a special tent in which God was worshipped in song 24/7. It was his passion and dream that God would live among people. He could see that a nation with God living at the centre of everything would be awesome. The people would prosper, the poor would be satisfied and people would be full of joy.[4] David went to great lengths to create the environment where the presence of God would be found at the heart of the nation, employing worship musicians to sing and play day and night.

We will take another look at David later.

Fast forward

This is where I have to slow down and breathe. Leaping forward to the New Testament, we read the famous account of how Jesus turned up at the river Jordan to join the multitude of people gathering to be baptised by his cousin, John. These crowds had been drawn out into the wilderness from surrounding towns and villages to see a wild-looking man, who was full of the Holy Spirit, preaching an uncompromising message of repentance. Then followed a brief discussion with John, who thought Jesus should be baptising him instead, but Jesus insisted that John go ahead and baptise him. Jesus won the argument. The newly baptised Jesus came up dripping from the water and was praying when the *heavens opened*, and the Holy Spirit descended in the form of a dove and settled on him. At that moment a voice boomed from heaven: 'This is my beloved Son, with whom I am well pleased' (Matthew 3:17).

If we do a bit of unpicking, we can see right here the same elements that were present in the story with Jacob. Let's say that Jesus is the rock (we will discover why as we go along, hopefully); he is the heaven-opener, plus the Holy Spirit is present in the form of a dove – completing the picture of the oil (oil is a metaphor for the Holy Spirit, as we shall see) poured on the rock – and God the Father, speaking from heaven, just as he had with Jacob.

This is an amazing scene: God the Father, delighting in Jesus the Son and anointing him with the Holy Spirit. Isaiah the prophet prophesied this, 700 years earlier: 'Behold my servant, whom I uphold, my chosen, in whom my soul delights; I have put my Spirit upon him; he will bring forth justice to the nations' (Isaiah 42:1). This is the Messiah-making moment: Father, Son and Holy Spirit all showing themselves together, heaven wide open – can you even imagine what John must have been thinking? 'I actually had my hands on the Messiah!'

Let's get back to the rock. Just for argument's sake, let us imagine this rock is a metaphor, or a prophetic picture, if you prefer, of Jesus. Jesus is the Christ; most definitely anointed by God. He is the true king, the rightful heir to David's throne; he is the true High Priest who will live forever, mediating the way for humanity to approach God.[5] He is the one who opened heaven to humanity. He made the kingdom of heaven accessible to the *ordinary* people, releasing its atmosphere of love and power for their benefit. As Jesus was born, a new epoch of spiritual history began; choirs of angels filled the sky singing, 'Glory to God in the highest, and on earth peace, good will toward men' (Luke 2:14 KJV). Like Jacob's pillar, Jesus was to stand on the earth, pointing the way to heaven. He now stands in heaven for all time: Jesus the heaven-opener.

Grumpy and undeserving

When the fledgling nation of Israel had miraculously escaped Egypt, supernaturally crossed the Red Sea and witnessed the mass drowning of the chariots and horses of Pharaoh, they parked up their flocks in the desert at a place called Rephidim and started grumbling. The feelings of elation and gratitude for the deliverance from their enemy had evaporated – God's people were now in a sour mood because they were thirsty. As was their habit, they turned on Moses and made it his fault! 'Why did you bring us up out of Egypt, to kill us and our children and our livestock with thirst? . . . Is the LORD among us or not?' (Exodus 17:3–7). Their thirst was a legitimate need, but their response was to doubt the God who, days before, had freed them from 400 years of slavery. In spite of their stinky attitude, this presented another miracle moment. Through each

successive supernatural intervention God was progressively
revealing himself to these people and, of course, to all future
generations, including us.

The Lord spoke to Moses, telling him to stand by the rock
at Horeb and give it a whack with his staff. (This was Moses'
special staff, previously used to perform the miracles in front
of Pharaoh and split open the Red Sea, to make a path dry
enough to cross over.) Moses obeyed and the rock gushed out
fresh water; the people and flocks drank and everyone was
happy again. This is a fabulous example of God's kindness to
ungrateful, undeserving people, but the story grows legs. The
time comes when the people are thirsty again. This time God
instructs Moses to take his staff, go with Aaron, in front of
the people, and *speak* to the rock. Moses is stressed and fed up
with the people and, instead of speaking to it as instructed,
hits the rock twice. The rock obligingly pours out water and
everyone can drink, but God is not happy. God rebuked Moses
and said that he would not be going into the Promised Land
after all. 'Because you did not believe in me, to uphold me
as holy in the eyes of the people of Israel, therefore you shall
not bring this assembly into the land that I have given them'
(Numbers 20:12).

As a child, hearing these stories, I always felt sorry for Moses.
Now, as a pastor, I have even more sympathy for him – worn
down as he was by grumpy people. In fact, God's rebuke of
Moses doesn't really make a lot of sense until we read the apostle Paul's comments on the story in his New Testament letter to
the Corinthians. Paul is teaching the Corinthian church from
Israel's history and recounts their escape from Egypt and journey in the desert under the leadership of Moses. He likens their

passage through the Red Sea to baptism, then goes on to speak of how they ate supernatural food, the manna and quail, and drank supernatural drink. 'For they drank from the spiritual Rock *that followed them*, and *the Rock was Christ*' (1 Corinthians 10:4, emphasis added). First, I am fascinated by the idea of a rock following them around the wilderness – that's amazing by itself! Then, what a stunning thought – the rock that Moses hit with his staff, which then poured out fresh water, satisfying a whole nation's thirst, was Christ – meaning, anointed – in fact, it was somehow Jesus! The heavenly makeup department did a great job of the disguise!

The eternal plan of God actually *required* that Jesus be struck, but only once: 'For Christ also suffered *once* for sins, the righteous for the unrighteous, that he might bring us to God' (1 Peter 3:18, emphasis added). It was necessary, to cover the cost of the sins of the human race, that the beautiful Anointed Christ should suffer and die at the hands of the people he created – but he should only be crucified once.

Unique friendship

Moses has always been in a league of his own in terms of friendship with God. God himself commented that he spoke with Moses face to face and not in riddles like he did with the other prophets. Moses spent so much face time with God that sometimes his own face shone so brightly that he had to wear a veil for days.[6] The more we see of Moses' unique relationship with God, the more we realise that he must have known something of Jesus – maybe he knew partially that there was something special about the rock and knew that hitting it was a bad idea.

In fact, the writer of the book of Hebrews states, 'He considered the reproach of *Christ* greater wealth than the treasures of Egypt, for he was looking to the reward' (Hebrews 11:26, emphasis added). He definitely was in on some special secrets.

Whilst Moses had been on the top of the mountain in the clouds of fire, receiving the Ten Commandments from God himself, the Israelite people had been busy making an idol in the shape of a calf. They had taken some of the gold they had been handed by the Egyptians as they were leaving Egypt in the wake of the plagues and given it to Aaron, Moses' brother. Aaron had been left in charge of the people for the forty days that Moses was in the cloud. Under his leadership the people had created the idol and begun to worship it, giving it the credit for leading them out of slavery. It does seem hard to believe! Moses had descended carrying the Ten Commandments, etched by the very finger of God on stone tablets. As he had approached the bottom of the mountain he heard the sound of dancing and celebration. When he saw the people of God cavorting in a drunken orgy he was furious and threw the tablets to the ground, where they smashed to pieces.

Not a good day.

Moses then returned up the mountainside a second time to meet with God to discuss the future – to see if Israel even had a future! We see Moses pleading with God; a mediator, or intercessor, fighting for the honour of God's name. Moses pleads with God not to annihilate the people because of their rebellion, but goes further – he begs God to accompany them on their journey personally, not just to send an angel to lead them. God's response is awesome: 'This very thing that you have spoken I will do, *for you have found favour in my sight, and I know you by name*' (Exodus 33:17, emphasis added). This is mind blowing! God has just spoken to a man and answered his request because he has found favour with God! Moses then seizes the opportunity and asks for the biggest prize he could think of.

Show me your glory . . .

Amazingly, God also grants Moses this request. In fact, we discover throughout the Bible that God absolutely loves it when we come looking for him. We read in the book of Hebrews that he is the rewarder of those who make the effort to seriously look for him.[7] In fact, he is the reward![8] God then explains how this encounter was going to work, making it clear that it was not going to be possible for Moses to see his actual face, because no-one can see his face and live.

Behold, there is a place by me where you shall stand on the rock, and while my glory passes by I will put you in a cleft of the rock, and I will cover you with my hand until I have passed by. (Exodus 33:21,22)

Moses then stands on a rock and watches as heaven is opened in front of him. The rock he is standing on is split, cut open – God hides Moses in the cleft to protect his humanity whilst exposing him to his glory. Jesus was split open; his physical body was split by the point of a Roman spear plunged into his side. Jesus, the Anointed Rock, is the fulfilment of Jacob's vision: he is the one who brings heaven to earth, he is the one we hide in and are safe as we encounter God.[9] Moses, hidden in Christ, the Rock, covered by the hand of God, watches as the glory of God passes by. What a moment!

To completely mix our metaphors, Jesus is the scuba mask which enables us to accurately see God. Without him we only see caricatures – a warlike vengeful god, or a passive inactive god – Jesus reveals Abba, the Father (more on that later).

Oil from the rock

Towards the end of his life Moses recounts God's love and care for the people of Israel during their time in the wilderness. In this profound poem found in Deuteronomy 32, he refers to God as the Rock.

For I will proclaim the name of the LORD; ascribe greatness to our God! The Rock, his work is perfect, for all his ways are justice. (verses 3,4)

You deserted the Rock, who fathered you; you forgot the God who gave you birth. (verse 18 NIV)

The language is so intimate:

And he suckled him with honey out of the rock, and oil out of the flinty rock. (verse 13)

This is profound! We come to God, the Rock that pours out refreshing sustaining water, and we find honey: honey is a metaphor for the Word of God; and oil, the Holy Spirit. As we dig into the Rock that is Jesus, we are fed and nurtured with revelation from God's Word, while the anointing of the Holy Spirit is released to us.

The Old Testament is so dense with layers of truth laid down like diamonds or seams of gold hidden in, well, rock! It is so worth the time spent digging!

Hiding place

David was chosen by God to be king of Israel whilst King Saul was still alive. Saul sensed that God's blessing and favour had left him and was now clearly resting on David. This, coupled with a tormenting demonic spirit, did not leave Saul feeling kind or generous towards David – instead he began to hunt him like a dog. David, meanwhile, found a great hideaway called the Cave of Adullam (see 1 Samuel 22:1). Near the valley of Elah, where he brought down Goliath, with a well-hidden entrance, it is big enough to fit forty people. This became David's home, his refuge and the destination of both runaway slaves and mighty warriors who came looking for refuge and found shelter under David's leadership at that time.

In many of the psalms written by David he refers to God as the Rock. He had learned to find refuge in God's presence. Imagine the conflict in David's heart as he runs for his life from the man God had originally chosen and anointed as king – his boss, in fact. The desire to be rid of the constant threat from Saul and his men like a pack of hounds, yet the sacrosanct sense of inner restraint which prevented him from harming Saul (more on this later). David had the deepest respect for the anointing. He understood that God's anointing made the person God's representative on the earth. He wrote Psalm 18 when he was fleeing from Saul:

> *The LORD is my rock and my fortress and my deliverer, my God, my rock, in whom I take refuge, my shield, and the horn of my salvation, my stronghold.* (Psalm 18:2)

> *Great salvation he brings to his king, and shows steadfast love to his anointed, to David and his offspring forever.* (Psalm 18:50)

David was God's chosen and anointed king, yet he learned to find his refuge in the Rock, the Anointed One. Like Moses, hidden in the cleft of the rock, encountering the glory of God first-hand, or Jacob with heaven opened before his very eyes, David became intimately close to God whilst sheltering in the cave.

Let's pause and reflect . . .

There is a lot going on in this chapter.

1. Why does God open heaven to a man such as Jacob? He had a lousy character, yet God granted him a backstage pass to see the invisible world of heaven. Was this:
   a. Because God is very kind and wanted to cheer him up?
   b. Because of the promises he had made to his grand-father Abraham?
   c. God might choose to do this for anyone?
   d. Another reason: (explain)
2. Ponder Jesus as the Rock for a moment. Where can you find biblical evidence of the following statements?
   - He is a place of safety.
   - He is the one who satisfies our thirsty soul.
   - He is the one who washes our wounds.
   - He is the one who gives us access to the riches of heaven.
   - We hide in him and see the glory of God.
   - He was beaten to release blessing.
3. The most important question of all:
   - Have you experienced the New Birth by coming to Jesus as defenceless as a child and surrendering your personal sovereignty to him?
   - Have you become aware of spiritual realities and an unseen realm which exists all around you? Was this gradually or suddenly?
   - Have you begun to experience his process of trans-formation in your heart, value system and priorities?

2: Negotiating Terms

olive oil

The term *the Anointing* seems to be largely monopolised by a certain slice of the church. The people who use this term tend to be the kind of people who believe in miracles, who talk about the tangible presence of God and believe in the present-day use of spiritual gifts such as prophecy, tongues and healing. *The Anointing* has become a classic piece of 'Christianese' – a jargon term owned by Christians and churchgoers, which gets dropped in to all kinds of conversations, such as those following a Sunday church meeting or a healing conference. It is not unusual to hear a preacher or worship leader described as anointed. It is, for some reason, less common to hear of a really anointed retail assistant or police officer.

Non-religious

The term *anoint* simply means to smear something on something, such as rubbing on ointment. However, in the context of Christianity and the Bible it's a big deal.

Religious

The practice of anointing with oil is very present in the more ancient branches of the church, such as the Catholic, Orthodox, Anglican and Episcopal churches, where oil is used to anoint people into the ordained ministry and as part of the ministry to sick people as instructed by the apostle James (James 5:14). Within such churches, anointing with oil is seen as an outward sign of God's active presence for healing or ordination. It is often combined with hands being laid on an individual who is receiving prayer for healing. Oil may be applied to the forehead in the sign of the cross on a person immediately after their baptism – this oil may have fragrance added depending on that particular church tradition. It is used as a representation of the Holy Spirit sealing the believer as mentioned in Ephesians 1:13,14:

> *In him you also, when you heard the word of truth, the gospel of your salvation, and believed in him, were sealed with the promised Holy Spirit, who is the guarantee of our inheritance until we acquire possession of it, to the praise of his glory.*

The Bible uses the Hebrew word *Mashach* in the Old Testament, meaning to smear, to rub over or paint. The New Testament uses the Greek word *Criō* which means to touch with the hand, or smear. From these two words we have the names *Messiah*, from the Hebrew *Mashiyach*, meaning anointed, and *Christ*, from the Greek *Christos*, which also means anointed. Jesus Christos/Mashiyach is Jesus, the Anointed One. For the purpose of this book I would like to launch the term the *Christing*. OK, so it's not officially a real word (yet), but I think it helps us to reframe our concept of the anointing. We are not thinking about a nice feeling we get during worship; we are thinking of the defining term which made Jesus of Nazareth the single most significant agent of change ever to grace the Blue Planet.

Special recipe

Whilst my wife was having a makeover in a cosmetic concession in a large department store, I slipped into a conversation with a salesperson about his secret passion, perfumery. The job running the cosmetics department was just a day job. He had created a number of unique fragrances and was in the process of making a name for himself as a master perfumer. I was stunned. He owns some ingredients that are so valuable that he keeps them in a safe. However, the most valuable asset to a master perfumer is a well-trained nose. The art of the perfumer was also vital in the Old Testament protocol for appointment of priests and kings. In the ceremony, a specially prepared anointing oil was poured over their heads. This oil was blended according to a unique recipe which was strictly limited in its use. This oil was a work of art in its own right – the work of a master perfumer.

> *Take the finest spices: of liquid myrrh 500 shekels, and of sweet-smelling cinnamon half as much, that is, 250, and 250 of aromatic cane, and 500 of cassia, according to the shekel of the sanctuary, and a hin of olive oil. And you shall make of these a sacred anointing oil blended as by the perfumer; it shall be a holy anointing oil.* (Exodus 30:23–25)

This oil was also used to consecrate, or set apart for exclusive use, the special ceremonial utensils used in worship ceremonies conducted in first the Tabernacle (tent) of Moses and then the Temple built by King Solomon. Everything to be used in the worship of God was considered sacred: specially belonging to God alone. These utensils had no other use but for facilitating the worship of God. Similarly, this oil was not available on the open market; it was God's secret recipe and he was jealous about its use. 'It shall not be poured on the body of an *ordinary person*, and you shall make no other like it in composition. It is holy, and it shall be holy to you' (Exodus 30:32, emphasis mine).

Aaron and his sons, then their sons after them, were reserved to be anointed as priests. The Old Covenant priesthood was a role given exclusively to Aaron and his boys. Years later, Saul and then David were chosen by God to be king of Israel. They were likewise anointed by the prophet Samuel to rule. The anointing as practised under the Old Covenant signified people that were emphatically *not ordinary people*. They were special, chosen by God and set apart from the ordinary. They even smelled different – unique. They were men set apart to act on behalf of God in the administration of his kingdom on the earth. It is also worthy of a note that under the Old Covenant that priests and kings were exclusively male. However, watch this space . . .

Transformational

Reading the Old Testament we can see that the anointing not only signified something, it also, on occasions, brought about an actual change in the nature of the person receiving the anointing. Saul was chosen to be the first king of Israel. The prophet Samuel anointed him with oil. This was followed by a powerful encounter with the Holy Spirit where Saul actually became a different person. 'The Spirit of the LORD will come powerfully upon you, and you will prophesy with them; and *you will be changed into a different person*' (1 Samuel 10:6, emphasis added). David similarly experienced a powerful infilling from the Holy Spirit following his anointing with oil. 'Then Samuel took the horn of oil and anointed him in the midst of his brothers. And the Spirit of the LORD *rushed upon David* from that day forward' (1 Samuel 16:13, emphasis added). We see an external symbolic act with a massive spiritual effect – in this case, the prophet Samuel takes a horn full of olive oil and pours it over the man chosen by God to be king; at the same time the Spirit of God *rushes on* that individual and infuses him with a supernatural power. The Holy Spirit is still the same; we will see that even in the New Testament he still rushes on people causing a profound transformation, sometimes in a moment.

The word *anointing* translated into Spanish is *unction*. This word also appears in English, mostly in relation to religious matters. But, to my mind, unction seems to convey a certain sense of something extra – more oomph, or vavavoom! Dictionaries usually define unction in connection to religious rites, such as we have mentioned above, but also add the dimension of divine influence coming over an individual, or an exhibition of spiritual inspiration or particular passion.

No guarantee . . .

Sadly, a reading of the books recounting Israel's history in the Old Testament illustrates graphically that receiving the anointing guaranteed neither good character nor, indeed, a successful reign. King Saul, for example, begins well, experiencing the genuine power of God in his life – he is a great leader initially – but soon starts making poor choices and parts company with the Spirit of God. Tragically, God ultimately rejects him and appoints David as a successor.

On our journey together, we will look at various of examples from the Old Testament and explore how the practice of anointing with oil relates directly to the gift of the Holy Spirit as poured out in the New Testament and beyond. It turns out that the anointing is a super-important theme, vital to the vitality of everyone who is a disciple of Jesus. This book is an attempt to unlock the treasure chest of scripture to help a generation discover the secret to life in the fulness of the precious Holy Spirit.

Let's put on our scuba mask and dive in: let's take a look at Jesus.

Let's pause and reflect . . .

1. Why do you think something as mundane as smearing was chosen to identify kings and priests and ultimately God's special envoy, Jesus?

2. Consider the idea of 'divine influence coming over an individual'. Do you think you have ever experienced such a thing in your own life, or have you ever seen it happen to another?

3. Have you ever used oil when you have prayed for a sick person's healing, or has it been used on you?

4. How might God's divine or spiritual influence transform your usual day?

3: Manifesto

The New Jesus

After forty days of absolutely no food – exposed to the heat of the sun, alone in the desert, whilst being tempted by the devil – Jesus turns up in the synagogue at Nazareth, his home town. It can seem that temptation is powerful and hard to resist, but for us, temptation is a result of our own sinful desires running away with themselves and demanding our attention (see James 1:14). Jesus, however, was tempted by the all-time temptation pro, Satan, also known as the 'father of lies'. He treated Jesus to a masterclass demonstration of his art; skilfully waiting until Jesus was worn out with hunger and fatigue before swooping in for the kill. It's not hard to imagine an audience of filthy sniggering demons picking their teeth, sitting around on the rocks, watching the show as their guy pulls out his best stunts. In spite of all this, Jesus coolly walks away unsullied – the undisputed champion.

Forty days before, Jesus had arrived at the river Jordan to be baptised by John. God had entrusted to John the historic responsibility and totally unique role of identifying the Messiah, or Christ, to the world. John himself was an amazing guy with an amazing story. His mother had been infertile and way past the age where having a child was a possibility. His dad was a priest, who was chosen by the drawing of straws as the privileged one

selected to offer smouldering
incense to God on a particular day. Whilst performing
this sacred duty he had a
surprise encounter with an
angel. The angel foretold the
miraculous birth of a son to

them in their old age and insisted that his name should be John
(Beloved). He went on to describe how this son would be filled
with the Holy Spirit from his mother's womb![1] We are told
very little about John's childhood, except that he grew strong
and had the favour of God on his life. He lived a secluded life
in the wild places eating a fab diet of locusts and wild honey!
Now suddenly he is catapulted into high-profile public
ministry – people from every strata of society now stream from
the towns and villages, into the remote wilderness to listen to
this emerging prophet. Speculation was rife about this unusual
man's true identity; people began to wonder if he was indeed
the Christ – a general expectation had developed amongst
devout Jews that a Messiah would eventually come, possibly
quite soon. John was definitely turning people back to a serious
relationship with God. But he insisted that another mightier
than he was coming: 'He [the One who is coming] will baptise
you with the Holy Spirit and with fire' (Luke 3:16, parenthesis
added).

We have already mentioned this moment in chapter 1: as Jesus
emerged from the water and was praying, the heavens were
opened and the Holy Spirit appeared in the form of a dove
and came down and settled on him. At that moment, God
the Father boomed from somewhere off-stage: 'You are my
beloved Son; with you I am well pleased' (Luke 3:22). This was

the game-changing moment for John. He now knew that his second cousin, Jesus, was indeed the Messiah. John had previously been given a clear indication from God that the sign of the true Messiah would be the one on whom he saw the Spirit descend and remain. 'I myself did not know him, but he who sent me to baptise with water said to me, "He on whom you see the Spirit descend and remain, this is he who baptises with the Holy Spirit"' (John 1:33). This very moment had just happened in front of his eyes. He knew that his purpose was now to step back and make room for the Christ to take centre stage.

Good news

Jesus, the local carpenter, apparently the son of Joseph, had been well known to the people of Nazareth, his home town, but this time he looked different. He had come into town from his desert showdown with the devil in the power of the Holy Spirit. It was the Sabbath, so he went to the synagogue, his normal Sabbath routine. He stood up to read from the scripture and was handed the writings of the prophet Isaiah. He scrolled down to the section we call chapter 61. (The chapters and verses in the Bible were added by monks for navigational purposes in the 16th century.) The New Testament writer, Luke, tells us the story in chapter 4 of his account of the gospel. However, I have taken the quote from the Old Testament:

> *The Spirit of the Lord GOD is upon me,*
>   *because the LORD has anointed me*
> *to bring good news to the poor;*
>   *he has sent me to bind up the broken-hearted,*

> to proclaim liberty to the captives,
>   and the opening of the prison to those who are bound;
> to proclaim the year of the LORD's favour,
>   and the day of vengeance of our God;
>   to comfort all who mourn;
> to grant to those who mourn in Zion –
>   to give them a beautiful headdress instead of ashes,
> the oil of gladness instead of mourning,
>   the garment of praise instead of a faint spirit;
> that they may be called oaks of righteousness,
>   the planting of the LORD, that he may be glorified.
> They shall build up the ancient ruins;
>   they shall raise up the former devastations;
> they shall repair the ruined cities,
>   the devastations of many generations. (Isaiah 61:1–4)

This is so cool! In reading aloud this portion of the scripture, Jesus was laying out his manifesto. He was saying, 'Hey, folks, this is why I'm here.' This first day of what we understand to be Jesus' adult ministry sets the scene for everything else he does during the next three years. He begins by explaining that his anointing is, in fact, a *person* – the Holy Spirit – all over him, like oil. Suddenly we begin to see that the anointing of priests and kings in the Old Testament was actually a shadowy picture of the anointing of the Christ. 'The Spirit of the LORD is upon me, because he has anointed (Christed) me to proclaim good news to the poor' (Luke 4:18, parenthesis added).

Bad news

Poverty is bad news. Delhi: a naked child sleeping on a concrete pavement, legs splayed wide, on view to every passer-by; her mother sitting staring vacantly into the middle distance with a toddler by her feet and baby asleep on her arm. This is poverty. This is bad news. It is bad news that the little girl's mum has lost all instinct to cover her little daughter's nakedness. It's bad news that her future will probably be an early career as a child prostitute; that her nakedness will be consumed by men who do not love her. Surely, anything remotely like good news to this mother must be that something is going to change for the better. Good news to the poor cannot merely be, 'You will remain poor, but don't worry, you will go to heaven when you die.' The good news we see in the gospel accounts is, something is now going to change because Jesus is here!

In the Law of Moses God commanded the Israelite nation to take care of the poor on purpose. 'For there will never cease to be poor in the land. Therefore I command you, "You shall open wide your hand to your brother, to the needy and to the poor, in your land"' (Deuteronomy 15:11). We only have to look at Jesus portrayed in the gospels to see that he consistently honoured poor people; he elevated them, loved their children, healed them, forgave them and set them free from life-controlling demonic oppression. Jesus was, and still is, phenomenally good news to the poor.

Not a sin

It is not a sin to be poor, any more than it is a sin to be broken-hearted, a captive or bound (some translations read 'oppressed'). In every context poverty is a result of the thieving activities of the devil. It affects us at the most basic levels of need. Food, shelter, security – poverty robs these from the lives

of its victims. Poverty means that in Maslow's famous hierarchy
of needs, luxuries such as self-actualisation and transcendence
never get a look in. Poverty is broken humanity trapped by the
absence of the bare necessities of life (and no singing bear). It
is precisely this brokenness which Jesus launches straight into.
For Jesus, it is an opportunity for the good news to transform
the world of human beings. It presents us, as disciples of Jesus,
with challenges which make us dig deep to find this anointing
which doesn't just create dependency cultures, but actually sets
people free from the grinding misery of lack.

When Jesus shows up, everything changes. It's the whole idea
behind the so-called Beatitudes. The Beatitudes is the name
given to a series of soundbites made by Jesus when he was
preaching to a crowd on the side of a mountain: the very famous
Sermon on the Mount. The assumption I made growing up in
church was that to qualify for blessing, we should be poor, hungry or weeping, as in Luke's account; or as Matthew says, poor
in spirit, mourning, meek, hungry for righteousness, pure in
heart, and so on.[2] I heard preachers describing the Beatitudes as
'beautiful attitudes', which reinforced this idea. However, what
I believe Jesus is saying is that wherever we find ourselves, whatever condition we are in, everything changes because he, the
Anointed One is here. In fact, Isaiah 61 is actually a preview of
the Sermon on the Mount written by a prophet called Isaiah
700 years earlier.

Rich in faith

It's really important, albeit slightly obvious, that the gospel –
the good news – is for the real world. It's not for some utopian

middle-class social experiment somewhere, where everyone knows the rules and knows how to behave. Jesus was very explicit to the self-satisfied religious experts who provided a running critique of everything he said and did: 'It is not the healthy who need a doctor, but those who are ill. I have not come to call the righteous, but sinners' (Mark 2:17 NIV). When Jesus speaks the blessing over the poor in Luke 6:20, he says, 'Blessed are you who are poor, for *yours is the kingdom* of God' (emphasis added). He is not making a generalised statement about poor people – out there, somewhere – he is actually addressing real people: you who are poor. They are sitting in front of him in the great multitude; he has just been healing them. Then he tells them how they are going to experience this blessing – he is giving them access to the kingdom of God. He is saying *yours is the kingdom* – to the poor. We are familiar with the tag at the end of the Lord's Prayer, often excluded from modern translations, 'For Yours is the kingdom and the power and the glory forever. Amen' (Matthew 6:13 NASB). This prayer is addressed to God the Father, but Jesus addresses the same thing to the poor: 'This kingdom is yours, with all its resources and privileges – I am giving it to you.' That is stunning!

The anointing of the Holy Spirit which rests on Jesus is transformative; revolutionary. James states: 'Listen, my beloved brothers, has not God chosen those who are poor in the world to be *rich in faith* and *heirs of the kingdom*, which he has promised to those who love him?' (James 2:5, emphasis added). Faith is the credit card which gives us access to the Father's account at the Bank of Heaven. Faith is the gift which ends poverty. The good news of Jesus turns the world upside-down. People who appear to be disadvantaged come to Jesus and find themselves boosted to the level of royalty.

Every place Jesus visited or passed through experienced good news. The life of each one he spoke to or touched was transformed: lives that were frozen, held in deadlock, like the man beside the miracle pool of Bethesda – he had been waiting there for thirty-eight years. From time to time a healing angel came and made the waters bubble up. Time and again, sick people more mobile than he, scrabbling frantically, dragged their broken, disfigured bodies into the water ahead of him and were miraculously healed. He, meanwhile, remained imprisoned in a severely disabled body; tantalisingly near to healing, yet never quite near enough. One encounter with Jesus and this guy no longer needs to get into the water – he's done! Healed! (See John 5:8.)

Something changes in a woman's life when, caught in the act of adultery, she is dragged and roughly thrown to the ground in front of Jesus by an angry lynch mob. The lawyers and religious experts are excited. They are eager to see Jesus line up squarely behind the law, giving his approval to the religious vigilantes to stone her to death. Or maybe he will not have the stomach for a stoning, so they can then accuse him of wimping out and betraying the law. Instead of getting sucked in to their sinister agenda, Jesus sits drawing pictures in the sand. He is so chilled and composed as he exposes the blatant hypocrisy in the hostile posse of accusers. In the end there is no-one left with an accusation against her. He sends her away unharmed and un-condemned to begin a new life.

Another day – more good news. Jesus and his band of disciples are invited to a wedding. Embarrassingly, the wine runs out long before the wedding is over. This is very bad news for the host who is afraid to dishonour his guests. Jesus, however, saves the party and the reputation of the host – turning the ceremonial foot-washing water into a cheeky little Shiraz – the best anyone had tasted. Such a non-Christian miracle to launch Jesus' miracle ministry – party on with Jesus!

Broken-hearted

Jesus and his interns arrive on the scene as a funeral procession passes by. The body of a young man is being carried to the grave. His mother, a widow, is among the mourners, wailing and lamenting his untimely death. This is such bad news – he had been the financial provider for this woman, now to be left destitute. Everyone who knows this woman, including some professional mourners, has turned up to add volume to the sound of tragedy. Jesus walks over to the bier . . . everything changes. The dead guy is no longer dead, his mum is laughing and kissing everyone – the funeral has now become a fiesta – because Jesus came! You start to get the feeling Jesus enjoys a good knees-up.

Imprisoned

Millions of people live trapped in many different kinds of prison. Some prisons are physical, with walls, razor wire and guards; others are prisons incarcerating people by fear and intimidation. Still others are captive to an addiction which controls their life and deprives them of the freedom to make good choices and to build a future. A fifty-four-year-old woman walked into the worship service at the Prayerhouse, our home church. She looked sad, but otherwise fairly 'normal'. After showing up for a few weeks, she told me how her second husband had recently tried to kill her by strangling and how her addiction to alcohol had wrecked two marriages. That Sunday, two years ago, she came into contact with the presence of God – in that moment the craving for alcohol just left. She has been free since then. That is good news!

All who mourn

Grief is an obsession. It is overwhelming, all-encompassing, exhausting; a dense blanket of energy-sapping fog with no visible way out. The horizon disappears; our plans, hopes and dreams all slip through our fingers like sand. Instead of the company of the one we love, our everyday companion is the dull, relentless ache of loss. Time does not always heal. It does dim the memories, but many never recover fully from the pain. Some cling to grief until it defines them, like Queen Victoria, who never changed from the black clothes of mourning after the death of her beloved husband Albert, until the day she died. However, according to Isaiah, the anointing of Jesus – the Christing – has the power to comfort *all* who mourn (Isaiah 61:2). This comfort is surely more than the well-meaning but bland sentiments expressed by kind people at times of death, such as, 'She's gone to a better place' and 'He's not suffering any more'. To be *really* comforted when we are *really* mourning would be a miracle. Exactly!

Isaac had been consumed with grief over the loss of his mother, Sarah. His father's chief servant had been gone many days on a quest to find his master's beloved son a bride. I imagine the crimson sun sinking low, casting long shadows across the desert; Isaac emerges from the tent as one of the servant boys runs into the camp excitedly shouting that Abraham's servant has

Abram's servant

returned. Isaac looks up and squinting in the evening light, sees the silhouettes of the camels approaching; his father's servant and the unmistakable figure of a young woman riding alongside. His heart races. As the caravan approaches, she modestly covers her lovely face with a veil. What a picture! The Bible is typically sparing on detail, but we sense the transformation of the atmosphere in Abraham's household with this delightful newcomer around, and the blossoming of romance between Isaac and Rebekah. We read: 'Then Isaac brought her into the tent of Sarah his mother and took Rebekah, and she became his wife, and he loved her. *So Isaac was comforted after his mother's death*' (Genesis 24:67, emphasis added).

Isaac was comforted because something fresh and lovely came into his grey and grieving world. His obsession with what he had lost was replaced with a new overriding obsession with what he had just gained. There was no way he could have his mother back. There was nothing but a collection of memories left for him in that particular relationship. But his future now suddenly looked exciting; full of promise, at the prospect of sharing it with this beautiful gift God had just placed into his arms.

When the anointing of the Holy Spirit that is on Jesus touches our lives it replaces our grief – our obsession with what we have lost – with something so awesome. It makes our future explode into life! When his anointing, the person of the Holy Spirit, touches us, anything is possible. For the widow at Nain, Jesus' unique version of comfort for her was to have her dead son returned to life. That's good news – the gospel, in fact. The good news is that *something is going to change, because Jesus has arrived*.

The point of this book is to make the good news that something is now going to change *because you or I have arrived*!

Putting the fun into funerals

A pastor friend of mine describes a scene where he was a guest at a funeral. The deceased was an elderly, godly man; both he and his widow had shared a great faith and hope in Jesus. My friend Clive had returned two days before from an overseas trip where he had been caught up in a major move of the Holy Spirit. Everyone he subsequently touched fell to the floor under the influence of God's love and power – fun, but not really the sort of shenanigans you expect at a respectable British funeral! On this occasion, however, Clive was trying to be on his best behaviour. The service now completed, one of the mourners turned to greet my friend, 'I hear you had a good time—' Let's just say, he *tried* to behave! He made the mistake of blowing gently on her and saying, 'Have some!' She slid to the floor between the pews! This, of course, caused a bit of a stir. The bereaved widow glanced over and realising what was going on, she too came over for a touch from the Holy Spirit! Seconds later, she was lying on the floor laughing helplessly, soon to be joined by the pastor who had conducted the funeral. When she regained her composure she remarked that if that was a taste of what her husband was now enjoying in heaven, she was very envious of him!

Beauty for ashes

The writer of Psalm 45 wrote a prophetic poem about Jesus, hundreds of years before his birth. It speaks of the oil of joy; literally, an anointing to be happy:

> *You have loved righteousness and hated wickedness. Therefore God, your God, has anointed you with the oil of gladness beyond your companions.* (Psalm 45:7)

Isaiah continues to describe the effect of the anointing of the Holy Spirit resting on Jesus. He describes the exchange of ashes for a beautiful headdress, or a crown of beauty: 'To give them a beautiful headdress instead of ashes, the oil of gladness instead of mourning' (Isaiah 61:3).

It was customary in Old Testament times to cover one's head in ashes as a sign of the depth of grief one was experiencing. Ashes are such a graphic metaphor for death. After a cremation, all that is left of the person we once may have loved, held in our arms and enjoyed for decades, is a small collection of dusty, lifeless ashes. However dearly we might hold those remains – maybe keeping them in pride of place in a special urn on the mantelpiece – they will never again kiss us, or laugh at our jokes; we will never again feel the warmth of their touch against our skin. Ashes are the reduction of a living thing down to its chemical components; stripped of life.

Ashes are a great metaphor for circular negative thinking – fruitless barren thoughts that simply cannot produce life, but rather cast the kiss of death over everything. We call this state of mind depression. Depression is a form of mental illness described by a psychiatric nurse friend as 'a bleak and grey existence'. Depression steals huge chapters of a person's life; closing down every bit of their creativity and spontaneity and reducing them to a shadowy form of themselves. Simply getting out of bed becomes a superhuman effort, leave alone actually achieving anything. J.K. Rowling said that depression isn't just being a bit sad; it's feeling nothing. It's not wanting to be alive anymore.

Miracle

This is the miracle: the anointing transforms a mind full of death and loss into something beautiful. The Holy Spirit, the brooding presence of God that exploded the whole universe into being, drips like oil from Jesus, restoring to life that which could never live. The Holy Spirit is the agent of resurrection – the very one who raised Jesus from the dead. Paul says, 'And if the Spirit of him who raised Jesus from the dead is living in you, he who raised Christ from the dead will also give life to your mortal bodies because of his Spirit who lives in you' (Romans 8:11 NIV).

Romans 14:17 could be paraphrased to read, 'Where God is in charge, living is not a set of rules about external things like food and drink, but a transformed life which pleases God, filled with miraculous peace and joy from the Holy Spirit.' It is important to remember that these qualities of joy and peace are supernatural. They come from a different source than our own natural resources. Jesus said to his disciples, 'Peace I leave with you; *my peace* I give you. I do not give to you as the world gives. Do not let your hearts be troubled and do not be afraid' (John 14:27, emphasis added). The world just cannot give this kind of peace. The peace that comes from Jesus is intrinsic to his nature – he is the Prince of Peace. He was the one peacefully snoring in the front of the boat during the raging storm whilst his friends fought desperately to keep the boat afloat. Jesus has no inner conflicts – he knows exactly who he is.

Let's pause and reflect . . .

1. Are there any situations that life presents which could not be transformed by a personal appearance of Jesus?
2. Think about your own context: family, work, place of study – do you represent good news to your spouse, children, siblings, colleagues, fellow students?
3. What particular storms are you facing at this time?
4. Is the peace inside you stronger than the storm on the outside?
5. Take a look at Psalm 103, particularly verses 4 and 5. 'Who redeems your life from the pit . . .' Do we naturally accept that illnesses like depression just take a long time to get over, or is there a promise here?
6. How can I realistically expect to comfort those who mourn without using bland platitudes?

4: Apart

Ownership

The Old Testament practice of anointing priests and kings had a lot to do with ownership. Quick history lesson: Jacob famously fathered twelve sons. The third son was called Levi. The men of the tribe which grew from his descendants were claimed by God and set apart for special duties. They became known as Levites. Two of his descendants (great-grandsons, by my calculations) were the famous brothers, Moses and Aaron. They were born to Hebrew slaves living in captivity in Egypt. Aaron became the first High Priest (not counting Melchizedek, more on him later) and his sons and grandsons and great-grandsons (etc., etc.) became the priesthood. These guys all belonged to God in a special way. They did not own land like the members of the other twelve tribes, nor were they allowed the same freedoms. God was their inheritance. They belonged to him and he belonged to them. Their work was taking care of the spiritual life of the community. They looked after the place of worship – this was initially the Tabernacle of Moses and subsequently the Temple – carrying out the sacrifices, prayers and ceremonial washing required by God. To take care of their own physical needs God set up the system of tithing. The rest of the nation gave a tenth of their profit from farming, both crops and livestock, to be income for the priests and Levites. The priests also got to eat from the meat that had been presented to God in offerings by their brothers.

And the LORD said to Aaron, 'You shall have no inheritance in their land, neither shall you have any portion among them. I am your portion and your inheritance among the people of Israel.' (Numbers 18:20)

The priests belonged to God and he, in turn, belonged to them. Because God was their inheritance, they really had no need for anything else. One of the names of God is El Shaddai, which is understood to mean God Almighty. He is the ultimate resource; everything is within his power to meet. As the priests gave themselves to him he fully sustained them, provided for them and kept them alive in body and soul.

This is the concept of *holiness*. It's another of those words which is used a lot in churchy conversations. Holiness is to do with being reserved and set apart for a special purpose. My eldest daughter was gripped by a passion to become a doctor from the age of nine when she was treated by an amazing plastic surgeon after a serious injury to her leg. (And yep, I was largely to blame for the injury.) From about this time in her life, once she finally recovered, each evening when she arrived home from school she went up to her room and put in an hour of study before the family meal. She did not watch TV in the evenings – she was busy studying. Leading up to her big exams, the walls of her room became entirely covered with meticulously hand-drawn, colour-coded diagrams of the digestive system, chemical reactions involved in respiration, cross sections of a human eye – it became a shrine to science exam revision. She set herself apart from much of the social life going on among her peers, even from just hanging out with the family. She became *holy*, set apart for her goal of becoming a doctor. (She's currently in her final year at medical school, so the strategy paid off.)

Cleanliness

The cardiac surgeon who performs a delicate operation on someone's heart will set herself apart for the purpose. She dresses in special clothes, covers her hair and spends an obsessively long time washing and scrubbing her hands and arms, before entering a spotless environment to carry out the procedure. The distance runner climbs out of bed whilst everyone else is asleep and pounds the dark, wet streets morning after morning. His friends stay up late and party, but he goes to bed early because he has to train in the morning. He sets himself apart from the chocolate muffin and a latte in favour of edamame beans and green tea. People tell him he looks skinny and that surely he can chill a bit, but when he stands on the podium wearing gold, it all seems worth it.

scalpel

Holiness is often considered in a negative light – as in, what holy people *cannot* do. For example, the priests and Levites were only allowed very limited contact with dead people – only a close family member. They were not allowed to have long hair or dreadlocks, but had to keep their hair tidy. They were not allowed to wear certain clothing. They had to be free from running sores and other yucky skin conditions involving pus. These rules seem super-picky and unnecessarily discriminatory to us, but God was making a point. Because they were anointed with holy oil and belonging to God, they were required to live a certain way. They were set apart to live in the environment of worship and the presence of God. Even the tongs and bowls and other items used in the sacrificial process were likewise anointed. They were made especially for use in the worship of God and were not to be used in any other context. The priest could not borrow a shovel from work to clear up after the dog or dig the garden!

Holy nation

Actually, God never just wanted a tribe of über-holy priests; what he was after was a holy nation.

> *Now therefore, if you will indeed obey my voice and keep my covenant, you shall be my treasured possession among all peoples, for all the earth is mine, and you shall be to me a kingdom of priests and a holy nation.* (Exodus 19:5,6)

He wanted a whole nation full of people loving him, talking to him and thinking of him when they were ploughing their fields or feeding the cattle. He wanted to be invited to be the answer to all of their prayers, the key to their prosperity. He wanted a nation of mums and dads bringing up their kids, teaching them how to be holy every day. Look at what he said about Abraham: 'For I have chosen him, that he may command his children and his household after him to keep the way of the LORD by doing righteousness and justice' (Genesis 18:19). He wanted the Israelite dads to tell their children the stories of his miraculous interventions on behalf of their nation – to instil a sense of identity as part of an entire people group belonging to God. God gave them a calendar with unique festivals designed by him to remind them of his dealings with them. Each year at the Passover feast each family was to re-enact a drama illustrating how their ancestors escaped from God's judgement against the Egyptian slavers, by slaying a lamb and smearing its blood on the door posts and lintel of their house. The youngest son was to ask the father what each element of the ritual meant. Over a meal of roast lamb – eaten standing up, wearing their shoes and coats – Dad reminded the whole family of God's supernatural deliverance: the story of the Exodus and the birth of a nation.

God chose the Israelite people in order to make an example of them in such a way that would attract the other nations to him. He wanted to bless them and shower his goodness and love upon them to such an extent that they made being his special people irresistible. It was working pretty well when the Queen of Sheba came to visit King Solomon. She had heard how great God was, but she wanted to see for herself. When she left she was utterly flabbergasted.[1]

A thousand years later, Peter writes to the church, still in its infancy, 'But you are a chosen race, a royal priesthood, a holy nation, a people for his own possession' (1 Peter 2:9). He takes the themes of God's relationship with the nation of Israel and begins to apply them to the church. He goes on to teach believers to live on the earth as temporary residents, abstaining from the passions of the flesh. As before, with Israel, God wants the church to now stand out and to be vastly, undeniably different from those living as enemies of God.

Mystery man

Priests and kings are very different roles. A priest acts as a mediator between God and human beings, whereas a king has authority to rule and bring order into society. In the story of Abram, whose name God later changed to Abraham, we are introduced to a mysterious figure about whom we know very little. What we do know just makes him all the more intriguing. He seems to be both a priest and a king.

Abram and his nephew, Lot, were both very successful nomadic herdsmen. God had blessed them both to such an extent that they could no longer easily occupy the same territory, so they decided to go their separate ways to create room for each other. The land was very fertile and productive in the valley, but a bit more rugged up in the hill country. They would each choose their preferred destination. Uncle Abram was a really good guy and let the younger nephew choose first. He chose the lush valleys, not surprisingly, leaving Abram to occupy the less promising hills. However, the easy life in the valley brought with it many temptations for Lot and his family. There were other inhabitants living there, who had built for themselves luxurious cities, but their lifestyles had become deeply toxic. Sodom and Gomorrah, in particular, became legendary for their sexual promiscuity and depravity. In due course Lot and his family were sucked in by the lure of city life.

The wealth of these cities had made them ripe for takeover and a hostile bid came in the form of four kings called Arioch, Chedorlaomer, Amraphel and Tidal. These were warlords; rulers of the people of Ellasar, Elam, Shinar and Goiim. They conquered the cities of Sodom and Gomorrah and three other cities in the same area. For a number of years they exacted tribute until, finally, the kings of Sodom and Gomorrah and three other kings grew tired of it and rebelled. The uprising, however, didn't go well at all. The warlords beat the pants off them and, along with many of the citizens of the cities, Lot, his family and all their flocks and herds were taken into captivity.

When news of Lot's fate reached Uncle Abram he mobilised his private militia. He had 318 men, all trained in warfare, who were part of his household – or business empire. That night they set off in hot pursuit of the four raiding kings and defeated them. They rescued Lot and his family and all their stuff. Abram's boys were some guys! That's the story, now here's the point: when Abram returned victorious from this battle he ran into our mystery man – Melchizedek. Melchizedek was a local king, the king of Salem (thought to be Jerusalem). He came out to meet Abram returning from his stunning victory with – wait for it – *bread and wine*. He then proceeded to bless Abram in the name of 'God Most High, possessor of heaven and earth' (Genesis 14:19). Abram then responded by giving the mystery man a tenth of everything. (This is the earliest mention of tithing in the Bible, by the way.)

The economical writer of the story tells us only that Melchizedek was King of Salem and priest of God Most High. Someone else, it would seem, besides Abram, was living in close relationship with God. Nice! This could be the end of the matter: that he was a king and a priest living at the same time as Abram. That is, except that the priesthood, as we know it, was not set up until the time of Moses, centuries later, which made him a kind of prototype priest. Then, years after Moses, King David brings Melchizedek's name up again in the words of a psalm in which he prophesies about the Messiah, the Anointed One:

The LORD has sworn and will not change his mind, 'You are a priest forever after the order of Melchizedek.' (Psalm 110:4)

He suggests that Melchizedek was a kind of eternal priest in a special category all of his own; well, he and Jesus, that is. Then centuries later, we are thrown a curve ball by the New Testament writer to the Hebrews. He opens up the mystery, but not enough to stop it still being a mystery! He tells us that the name Melchizedek (the Hebrew is Malkiy-Tsedeq) means King of Righteousness, and that he was also the King of Salem, which means 'peace'. So he is the King of Righteousness and King of Peace and a special kind of priest. He then tells us that this enigmatic character has neither mother or father, nor will he die: 'He is without father or mother or genealogy, having neither beginning of days nor end of life, but resembling the Son of God he continues a priest for ever' (Hebrews 7:3). He is said to resemble the Son of God, in fact, his names sound very much like the names of Jesus listed by Isaiah.[2] (I often wonder where some of the New Testament writers get their bits of extra background information.)

Far superior

Hebrews, the letter addressed to the ethnic Hebrew followers of Jesus, makes the point that the person giving the blessing is superior to the one receiving (Hebrews 7:7). This certainly was the case in the Old Testament examples of blessing – we will think about this some more later in this chapter. What he is saying is that the greatly revered Hebrew patriarch, Abraham, was somehow lower in the food chain than Melchizedek. He then gets quite technical and explains that the father of the priesthood (which is still to come) – that is Levi, a son of Jacob, Abraham's grandson – was actually 'in the loins' of Abraham at this time. Not only so, but that he paid tithes to Melchizedek through his great grandfather.

The main point that the writer is making, is that somehow this priesthood represented by our mystery man, is much better than the Levitical priesthood instituted by Moses and would in due course replace it. This superior priesthood is also a *kingship* with a rule characterised by righteousness and peace; but also where *the priests never die*. He uses the psalm we referred to earlier to show that God's intention to replace the temporary priesthood with something better was prophesied centuries earlier than Jesus, by David. 'You are a priest forever after the order of Melchizedek' (Psalm 110:4). The *You* here is Jesus. Some believe that Melchizedek was, in fact, an Old Testament appearance of God or, indeed, Jesus. This would certainly explain the fact that his priesthood never ends. The writer to the Hebrews tells us emphatically that Jesus is now the High Priest of a much superior covenant.[3] Incidentally, if you are worried about the principle of tithing, or giving a tenth of your income to God – some argue that it belonged to the Law and upheld a now obsolete priesthood – the high priest without beginning or end received the tithe from Abraham, the father of faith, and the father of the priesthood. The tithe belongs to Jesus.

Initially, Melchizedek appears to have only a passing significance in the story of Abraham, other than to bless him and receive his tithe. However, he imparts a key revelation to Abraham, which in due course becomes ours too. He refers to God as, *God most High, possessor of heaven and earth*. This is loudly echoed by the apostle Paul in his letter to the Colossians.[4] He also appears as an *archetype*, a first mention of the priesthood of which the sons of Aaron would be a representation. This intriguing character is such a powerful foreshadowing – a prophetic signpost pointing to Jesus, our Great High Priest – that the Holy Spirit refuses to leave him out of the narrative.

Relentless

The Levitical priests were the go-betweens, serving God and serving the people, which was great, but everything depended on the slaughter of sheep, goats and cattle as sacrifices. It was relentless: sacrifices for sin, sacrifices to demonstrate love, sacrifices to say thank you, blood and guts, day in day out, year in year out – then there were the grain offerings. The whole thing was gory, messy and the constant smell of burning meat must have been pretty hectic. I love it when David says, 'For you will not delight in sacrifice, or I would give it; you will not be pleased with a burnt offering' (Psalm 51:16). The writer to the Hebrews picks up another Old Testament reference to the temporary nature of the sacrificial laws: 'Sacrifices and offerings you have not desired, but a body you have prepared for me' (Hebrews 10:5 and Psalm 40:6). The bloody brutality of sacrifices was a graphic illustration to the Israelite nation of what a nightmare sin is. Sin always brings death. In this case it was the butchery of countless innocent animals who had no quarrel with God. It would ultimately be the death of the sinless, entirely innocent God the Son, Jesus – the Christ, Anointed, Messiah.

Jesus, then, is the perfect King and the once-for-all-time High Priest, who is also the Lamb that was given in sacrifice as a once-for-all-time payment for sin – everyone's.

Royal Priests

But you are a chosen people, a royal priesthood, a holy nation, God's special possession, that you may declare the praises of him who called you out of darkness into his wonderful light. (1 Peter 2:9)

Just as Jesus is a priest and a king, we, too, because of his anointing on us, get to share in this awesome two-fold ministry. Historically, there has been a massive hijack of the ministry of priests within the church, since it became popular belief that priests were different to normal believers. This is just poor theology which became accepted by the majority and stuck. It is one thing to say that the pastor has a special call to lead the church, but another thing to say that he or she has a unique, exclusive role as a go-between for God and the *ordinary* people.

It's easy to see how people, and particularly scholars, read about the Old Testament priests and saw that the anointing was not to be used on an *ordinary* person.[5] This can lead to a conclusion that only *special* people can be priests. Five hundred years ago, in the Reformation, a revelation dawned which certain people dared to believe – that each genuine believer in Jesus actually is a priest. This was shocking, but awesome. It transformed the lives of many and has resulted in countless millions coming to Jesus through the regular Joes and Joannes, who had never once darkened the door of a seminary. However, even today, there is still a residual belief hanging around in the form of a clergy/laity divide. This has its roots back in the Old Testament, where priests were special and had an access to God that the non-priests did not. Or did they?

Enoch walked with God, then one day God invited him to stay at his place – he did not die – he was transferred into heaven. He was not a priest. Abraham was a friend of God. He became known as the father of all who believe. He was not a priest. Moses saw God's glory and spoke with him face to face. He was not a priest. David knew God intimately and set up 24/7 worship. He was not a priest. Daniel saw visions and interpreted dreams; he was an exceptional intercessor and led three pagan world leaders to faith in God. He was not a priest. We could go on. God has always been there for people to find. The priest's job was to be there to help people find him. Under the provisions of the law they were freed from certain pressures of life to be able to serve God and the people better, but they did not have *exclusive* rights to knowing God. Throughout history there have been countless examples of *non-official* priests – ordinary people have enjoyed an intimate friendship with God which has gone on to have a huge impact on other people. Katherine Kuhlman was a healing evangelist who rose to prominence in 1940s America. Many were healed in her crusades (she also had many critics). The atmosphere in her meetings was likened by those who attended to being in heaven. This quote is from a recent biography:

> *'You have been called "hypnotic, charismatic, hypnotizing,"' said Johnny Carson on* The Tonight Show *in 1974. His guest resisted. With a disarming smile, she said she was 'just the most ordinary person in the world.' Carson didn't buy it. 'You're not quite ordinary.'*[6]

What about us?

Peter makes some great statements, for example, look at this: 'Do not repay evil with evil or insult with insult. On the contrary, *repay evil with blessing*, because to this you were called so that you may inherit a blessing' (1 Peter 3:9 NIV, emphasis added). This is not just a nice way to live – be kinda nice and let people be – this is spiritual warfare. This is actively taking the victory of Jesus on the cross and rolling it out onto the streets. Jesus suffered the merciless abuse and insults of the soldiers carrying out his execution without any retaliation. As Isaiah prophesied: 'He was oppressed and afflicted, yet he did not open his mouth' (Isaiah 53:7 NIV). This is offensive warfare priesthood; we take the blessings of being loved by God, adopted into his family and anointed with his beautiful priestly anointing, which gives us privileged access to his presence, and then we release them into a petty, squabbling, broken world where beggars and orphans fight over a crust of bread – or a parking space.

Intercessory prayer could be described as bringing the needs of an individual or a community to God and representing them to him, whilst prophecy is standing near to God, catching his love and hearing what he is saying to individuals and communities, and then speaking it out to them. Blessing is different again. It is standing in the presence of God, discovering our position of immense favour, then using *our creativity and imagination* to speak out, releasing that favour to bring a miracle of transformation to an individual or community. Blessing is given at *our discretion*. It's like a rich kid who has her parent's credit card taking all her friends out on a shopping spree. Blessing works properly when we know who we are and who our daddy is!

Blessing is powerful and transformative; we invoke the intervention of God the loving Father into broken earthy situations. Take yesterday – as we speak, I am staying in an Airbnb in Toronto as I am attending a conference. It's cheap, budget basement accommodation – don't judge me for being a cheap-skate! The walls of my room are very thin and acoustically transparent. The other side of the wall is the kitchen. From about 1.30 a.m., the night before last, George, a fellow occupant, began preparing food – or something – in the kitchen, which took him at least two hours. The procedure required multiple trips to the refrigerator with multiple door slams, along with many unsuccessful attempts to programme the microwave, with beeps from the buttons and groans from the operator when the attempts failed. At one point it sounded as if all of the shelves in the refrigerator and their contents fell out on to the floor accompanied by more groans and expletives. On more than one occasion George himself crashed into the wall. I couldn't sleep – I simply lay there in the dark trying to imagine what drama might unfold next. Finally, at 4.00 a.m. I decided to make myself a cup of tea. I joined George in the kitchen. 'Bad night?' I asked. 'Yeah, I don't seem to be sleeping too well lately.' 'No kidding,' I thought.

Mysteriously, my milk had vanished from the fridge too.

'OK,' I thought, 'here's a chance to make this stuff work.' I went to war. Back in my room, under my breath, I blessed my insomniac flatmate with really good sleep and forgave him for sentencing me to dry granola for breakfast. The next night I slept undisturbed right through until 5.30 a.m. when I was awakened by a call from a law firm in London, who had not kept up with my itinerary. George, interestingly, did not appear in the kitchen until about 9.00 a.m. 'How was your sleep?' I asked. 'Actually, I slept really well,' he replied. I confess to feeling a small degree of smugness. Although there was some definite self-interest involved, my blessing was definitely a blessing to George.

This is radical, revolutionary stuff. In the Old Testament, the priests were supposed to be the ones giving out the blessings,[7] but now it's *our* job. We should not leave it to the vicar, or the person who stands at the front of church; let's reclaim the amazing role of priests and reclaim the words God spoke through Malachi to the sons of Aaron:

> *My covenant was with him, a covenant of life and peace, and I gave them to him; this called for reverence and he revered me and stood in awe of my name. True instruction was in his mouth and nothing false was found on his lips. He walked with me in peace and uprightness, and turned many from sin. For the lips of a priest ought to preserve knowledge, because he is the messenger of the LORD Almighty and people seek instruction from his mouth.* (Malachi 2:5–7 NIV)

Jesus is the single most amazing example of what a priest is supposed to look like. He was a super-busy guy. He was being pursued by people who wanted him to heal them of all kinds of diseases and conditions, he was being constantly watched and scrutinised by those who wanted to trap him by something he said, he was even being hunted by sinister people who wanted to kill him. He had plenty going on. That's why his disciples tried to keep the mums away when they brought their children to him for a blessing. We know the story: he rebuked his disciples and took the small children in his arms and blessed them.

I love Jesus. He jumped at the opportunity to speak something different into the hearts of the children to the lies they usually grow up hearing. He spoke from the position of the rich kid with the credit card. He wrote cheques that the Bank of Heaven would have delight in honouring. How about you and me? We can go around being gloomy about social evils, agreeing how terrible knife crime is among young people, complaining about teenage abortion rates, or we can start to bless the friends of our teenage children when they come to our home. We can start writing cheques on the Bank of Heaven account when we coach the local youth football team; we can bless those young people who hang out by the subway drinking cheap cider – alternatively, we could just agree with the devil and repeat the kind of stuff he is saying.

Earthmovers

In the late 1700s a man called Joseph Bramah developed a system of multiplying force based on the non-compress-ible nature of liquids. His hydraulic pump became the basis of a massive techno-  logical breakthrough with countless modern applications, such as hydraulic presses for shaping steel or the disc brakes on our cars. Thanks to this revolutionary discovery, an operator may now sit in an air-conditioned cab listening to music on the radio whilst lifting tonnes of dirt by pushing small levers, and without even breaking into a sweat. There is a Volvo quarry digger that can lift over 13 tonnes in one bite. So cool! When we bless, or forgive, we actually change the shape of the land-scape by pushing levers. One time, I was teaching on forgive-ness in the church. A few days later, one of the leaders came to me and told me how as a young person she had a bad relation-ship with her half-sister. She now lived in Australia and they had not spoken for many years. After realising that forgiveness neither means making excuses for the person, nor saying that the offence did not matter, she proceeded to speak out a declaration of forgiveness to her sister. Her sister was not present, neither did she consciously know anything of what was going on, but this lady spoke out loud as if she was. She understood that forgiveness is like ending a legal contract – it needs to be formally ended by word of mouth. The next day, the estranged sister, out of the blue, called her. They spoke warmly on the phone and enjoyed reconciliation. Sally had 'pulled a lever' called forgiveness remotely from the comfort of her own home in England and shifted a tonne of dirt in Australia.

If you forgive

Hopefully, if you are reading this as a Christian, you will have already become skilful and speedy at forgiveness! Forgiveness is not an option, it's part of our basic priestly kit. Because of Jesus we have experienced God's forgiveness, and not just once, we go on needing it pretty frequently. Surprising, therefore, that probably the number-one issue holding sincere followers of Jesus back from making progress is forgiveness. Just for a recap, in his world-famous prayer lesson, Jesus taught us to pray, 'And forgive us our debts, as we also have forgiven our debtors' (Matthew 6:12).

> *Jesus said to them again, 'Peace be with you. As the Father has sent me, even so I am sending you.' And when he had said this, he breathed on them and said to them, 'Receive the Holy Spirit. If you forgive the sins of any, they are forgiven them; if you withhold forgiveness from any, it is withheld.'* (John 20:21–23)

Jesus seemed to land in trouble with his religious critics again and again for one thing or another. On one occasion he forgave a man's sins as part of his healing process.[8] That went down badly with the scribes, who thought he was blaspheming – presuming to forgive sins – surely that is God's exclusive right. Well, I guess they would have been equally upset by this instruction to his disciples to forgive people's sins. There are the sins which are committed against us personally, well that makes sense that we should forgive, as mentioned in Matthew 6, but it doesn't stop there. Some political leaders make poor decisions which affect whole communities. Gangs draw young people into a culture of drugs and violent crime. Successive generations may adopt a poverty spirit in a particular neighbourhood. These are corporate sins which shape culture. It may be that generations earlier hostility sprang up between two parts of the community and the division is there today. We do not have to just accept the way things are with a resigned shrug and try to move to a better neighbourhood, we are the anointed priests of God and have an anointing to bring good news to the place where we live. We are called to forgive on behalf of the wider community and God will respond in heaven.

And I tell you, you are Peter, and on this rock I will build my church, and the gates of hell shall not prevail against it. I will give you the keys of the kingdom of heaven, and whatever you bind on earth shall be bound in heaven, and whatever you loose on earth shall be loosed in heaven. (Matthew 16:18,19)

I think Jesus believes in his disciples more than we believe in ourselves. Just sayin'! We will talk more about the whole *binding* thing in the next chapter.

Let's pause and reflect . . .

1. Do we assume that there is a priestly hotline to God – like the Batphone – that we as an ordinary member of the public do not have? Do we use that sneaky lie to justify our distance from God?
2. Review the past week. Have there been opportunities to release the spiritual warfare missile of blessing? How did you respond – with blessing or cursing? Or 'Christian' grumbling?
3. Have you become super-speedy at forgiveness, or do you:
   - grumble and complain a lot first?
   - mentally rehearse speeches that you want to say to the person who has wronged you?
   - plot revenge?
   - employ passive aggressive strategies to let the person know that you are offended?
4. How does forgiveness satisfy the need for justice to be done? Can we forgive someone who is not sorry?
5. How might we forgive the shapers of society, such as politicians, local council leaders and religious leaders on behalf of the nation, or a community?

6. Here is a useful declaration of forgiveness to be spoken
   out loud as if you are addressing the person (it can help
   to visualise the person you are forgiving and imagine
   they are in the room):

Name............................,

When you .... you wounded me.

Describe how. For example, *'You missed all of my birth-
days, ballet shows and parents' evenings at school. You were
never present to support me . . .'*

Don't rush, allow yourself time to catch up with the
emotional impact of the wound. Don't start making excuses for the person either!

*Today, however, I am giving you a gift you do not deserve.
I give you the gift of my forgiveness. I choose to completely
release you from the debt, to no longer hold you responsible
for how I am. I choose to no longer recycle this pain and
resentment towards you. I tear up the charge sheet against
you; you owe me nothing.*

There are various things you can do to help you connect
with the process, and make it memorable, such as write
a list of just how the wounding has negatively affected
you and tear it up, burn it, or write it on a helium bal-
loon and let it go. (Not very environmentally friendly,
that one!)

5: Executive Power

As a citizen of the United Kingdom, I am also a subject of Her Majesty Elizabeth the Second, by the Grace of God, of Great Britain, Ireland and the British Dominions beyond the Seas, Queen, Defender of the Faith. Our Queen is an amazing person to have as the head of a nation and I love hearing her share her faith with the English-speaking world on TV at Christmas. She is a modern-day monarch of a democratic nation. She does have certain constitutional powers, but most of her power has to do with her great personal influence. Her rule is not to be remotely compared with the power wielded by the kings who appear on the pages of the Bible. These guys had absolute power and ruled by decree. On the one hand they could be gracious and godly, or on the other, hideous despotic tyrants, but they were all to be greatly feared. The book of Proverbs wisely advises: 'A king's wrath is a messenger of death, and a wise man will appease it' (Proverbs 16:14).

The Bible pictures the king as an anointed servant of God with delegated authority to rule on the earth. David is the all-time number-one king of the nation of Israel. He is held up throughout the subsequent chequered history of the nation's monarchs as a paragon demonstrating the kind of kingship God was pleased with. Somewhat surprisingly, the Bible, even the New Testament, upholds the idea that monarchs are God's servants;

even the bad guys. Nero, the baddest of bad guys, was emperor at the time Paul wrote these famous words:

> *For rulers are not a terror to good conduct, but to bad. Would you have no fear of the one who is in authority? Then do what is good, and you will receive his approval, for he is God's servant for your good. But if you do wrong, be afraid, for he does not bear the sword in vain. For he is the servant of God, an avenger who carries out God's wrath on the wrongdoer.* (Romans 13:3,4 emphasis added)

I am not interested in attempting to justify bad leadership, or to advocate the return to a particular type of ancient monarchy, but rather to think about what kingly authority might mean to us in our dual anointing as kings and priests. God's design for leadership is that it should uphold justice and defend the weak, whilst bringing peace and prosperity to the nation and its neighbours. The best examples of kingship in the Old Testament did exactly that, but each successful king personally submitted to God's rule first. None of these succeeded by being unusually smart or courageous in themselves. Even the legendary wisdom of Solomon was a gift given to him by God.

Mind-boggling

There is a New Testament Greek word used to describe the authority given to those who believe in and surrender to the rule of Jesus: *exousia*. It has a big meaning: the power to choose, or to act independently; it can mean an endowment of power or strength, the power and authority of government, and can mean spiritual authority and authorities.[1] People reported that Jesus taught as one having *exousia*.[2] It was so noticeably different to anything coming from the contemporary religious leaders, that he naturally attracted a following. In Matthew 10, when Jesus called the twelve disciples, he gave them *exousia* over the unclean demonic spirits, to kick them out of people's lives. When Pilate was discussing the possible execution of Jesus, Jesus politely pointed out to him that whilst he may have been the Roman Governor, he had no *exousia* over Jesus other than what had been given to him by God. In fact Jesus said that he (Jesus) had *exousia* to lay his life down and to pick it up again.[3] So cool!

I have a friend who served for a number of years as a motorcycle cop in Wales. He also rode his own motorbike to and from work. On one occasion he was travelling to work using the motorway, when his bike broke down. He pulled over onto the hard shoulder, parked his machine safely, then stepped into the flow of traffic and held his hand up. A vehicle pulled over, he said to the driver 'Take me to Swansea police station please.' The motorist pleasantly let him into his car and duly drove him to the police station as requested. It was only as he thanked the driver and stepped out of the vehicle that my friend realised that he was dressed in civilian clothes. He was so used to taking authority, *exousia*, which was backed up by his uniform, that on this occasion, the person he pulled over responded to the aura of authority automatically – he did not even question my friend's right to make such a bold request of him.

Paul describes how Jesus has been raised to the highest level of authority far above every other authority anywhere, earthly or cosmic:

> *According to the working of his great might that he worked in Christ when he raised him from the dead and seated him at his right hand in the heavenly places, far above all rule and authority and power*

(exousia) *and dominion, and above every name that is named, not only in this age but also in the one to come.* (Ephesians 1:19–21, parenthesis added)

Here's the more outrageous part: Paul goes on to say that we mere humans have been raised and seated with the Anointed One in heavenly places – that is, elevated to be seated alongside Jesus in the rulership of the earth: 'And God raised us up with Christ and seated us with him in the heavenly realms in Christ Jesus' (Ephesians 2:6 NIV). I sometimes listen to myself talking about these things and it sounds incredibly grandiose – my natural inclination is to down-grade my status – maybe it's British false modesty, or just plain unbelief, and then I come back to the scriptures and realise it is for real. God really does lift up we, the most unqualified, and transport us to this place of cosmic influence. This is truly mind-boggling! When I think of all the stuff Jesus knows about me, I can only marvel at the thought that he might want me anywhere near anything important! He does not just rescue us from poverty, but seats us with princes.

Prototype

King Saul was plucked out of obscurity by Samuel the prophet and given the top job. He was anointed with oil, and in that anointing moment the Holy Spirit rushed onto him and transformed him into a different man. Shortly after, he found himself spontaneously prophesying along with the local prophets – the anointing he received was not just a ceremonial ritual, it was a transformational encounter with the Holy Spirit. Saul went on to become a champion who brought to the nation of Israel victory over their enemies and helped them form into a unified kingdom. He led major spiritual reforms, banning idolatry and witchcraft from the land. He was a good guy, who began well. Eventually, however, the hidden issues in his heart caught up with him, leading to his downfall. He was needy – constantly craving the validation from people. In fact, it was so important to Saul to have approval from his subjects that he chose it over approval from God. It is tragic that history remembers Saul as a failure, rather than as a success. I am always deeply saddened to hear of men and women, clearly anointed by God, who have become victims of their own unhealed hearts.

In Saul we see the first example of biblical kingship, apart from, possibly, Adam and Eve. Adam and Eve had been given authority from God to rule over all creation, but ended up settling for a piece of fruit instead. In that action of independence from God, they twisted their rightful *exousia* into rebellion. God had gifted them with freedom of choice which meant their rule on the earth would be expressed at their own discretion and with their own style and flavour. Tragically for the human race, they succumbed to the temptation as pitched by Satan: 'For God knows that when you eat of it (the forbidden fruit) your eyes will be opened, and you will be like God, knowing good and evil' (Genesis 3:5, parenthesis added).

In the examples of both Adam and Eve and Saul, the order and blessing which God desired on the earth was to be dispensed through human beings. It was God's idea to give us authority to act on his behalf. If we think back to Jesus' Luke 4 manifesto we discussed in chapter 2, we read that he is anointed 'to proclaim liberty to the captives, and the opening of the prison to those who are bound; to proclaim the year of the LORD's favour, and the day of vengeance of our God' (Isaiah 61:1,2). This is truly kingly behaviour: declaring to prisoners they are now free to walk out of their place of incarceration. It's a product of the Christing. We are Christed to bring an end to oppression, to set people free and to write cheques on the heavenly bank account, because God has declared a day of vengeance. He is coming after his enemies, the oppressors, with a big stick!

The big stick – the executors of God's vengeance – is you and me, God's Christed ones, driving back the powers of oppression and setting Satan's captives free. Jesus sent out his disciples with the words:

> *All authority* (exousia) *in heaven and on earth has been given to me. Go therefore and make disciples of all nations, baptising them in the name of the Father and of the Son and of the Holy Spirit, teaching them to observe all that I have commanded you. And behold, I am with you always, to the end of the age.* (Matthew 28:18–20, parenthesis added)

All authority means, *all authority*. The Christing does not mean that we get issued with a fancy-dress soldier's outfit, where we just look the part – we get the whole kit, a proper badge and a (don't worry, dear English people, this is a metaphor) gun – we have the full authority, or *exousia* of Jesus. But it's even better than that, Jesus says: 'And behold, I am with you always, to the end of the age.' In the epic *Lord of the Rings*, the unimpressive little furry-footed Hobbits are entrusted with the most daunting task which is vital to the future of the entire Middle Earth. It involves facing extreme perils like giant spiders and enemies who look like demons. The friends are accompanied for part of the journey by Gandalf, the wizard. He is very cool, as he is able to do magic, which often serves to get them out of trouble. But then at an apparently crucial time, he leaves them whilst he goes off to fight some evil beast, and the miniature heroes are very much alone. The awesome thing about the Christing is that the Holy Spirit, who is the Christing, is the Spirit of Jesus. Jesus himself is with us for the duration of the journey. Not only do we have his authority and power, but we have access to his wisdom and knowledge and the comfort of his presence. Not without reason is the Holy Spirit called the Comforter.

Showdown

John Wimber talked of demon eviction and healing people as *power encounters*.[4] These are moments when the anointing – the person of the Holy Spirit – confronts the spiritual power that has been in control up to that point. He brings a holy confrontation between the powers of darkness and the kingdom of heaven. This is Spiritual Warfare #101. Jesus said, 'But if I drive out demons by the finger of God, then the kingdom of God has come upon you' (Luke 11:20 NIV). Jesus demonstrated kingly *exousia* everywhere he went, but as we have just read, he commissioned his disciples to do the same. When we walk in the kingly anointing we can expect the demonic squatters around the neighbourhood to get uncomfortable and start reacting to our presence. This can be a little embarrassing when you have attempted to be incognito but the local demons know who you are.

It does often seem that the task entrusted to us by Jesus is so far beyond us. For example, if we were left to try to figure out how to heal someone without studying for a medical degree, we would probably take a really long time to become successful and have more than a few patients die as a result of our attempts. The good news is that we are not expected to be experts – or even to heal people by our own life force, or mystical power; the Holy Spirit does it through us – it is a miracle of the anointing. After Peter and John healed the severely disabled guy at the Beautiful Gate, a crowd gathered around them in amazement. Peter had to ask them, 'Men of Israel, why do you wonder at this, or why do you stare at us, as though by our own power or piety we have made him walk?' (Acts 3:12).

For a Western Christian living today it is easy to fall into approaching healing from a beggar's perspective, rather than a kingly one – begging for a crumb of healing from God, rather than delivering a miracle. Even if we are not medically trained, we do know quite a bit on an anecdotal level about various illnesses and conditions and likely outcomes, which can be quite intimidating. It might be worth pointing out, however, that a miracle is a miracle – a 'small miracle' is equally impossible as a 'large' one. Jesus, as far as we read, did not really pray for people to be healed, instead, he spoke the words and the healing happened. Often we hear prayers like, 'Oh God, here is dear Mavis, Lord, we bring her before you now, God. Lord, you know her heart, she really loves you, Lord, right now we lift her up to you. We ask for you to heal her leg, Father God, we ask you Lord, if it's your will . . .' It's easy to be so intimidated by the condition we see in front of us that we start to hedge our bets and try to give God (and ourselves) a get-out. It's important that we never forget who actually does the healing, but Jesus *commanded* us, 'Heal those who are ill, raise the dead, cleanse those who have leprosy, drive out demons. Freely you have received; freely give' (Matthew 10:8 NIV).

Pray at home

Challenging! It seems to me that it's too late to pray when I am confronted with the need – it is much more smart to do my praying every day so that I am full of the Holy Spirit and very oily before I leave the house in the morning. Then I can trust in the freshly poured anointing. Jesus frequently spent the night in prayer, or retreated to the wild places just to get some time in close contact with heaven. He was never caught unprepared, without the person of the Holy Spirit covering him.

Rebuilding

They will rebuild the ancient ruins and restore the places long devastated; they will renew the ruined cities that have been devastated for generations. (Isaiah 61:4 NIV)

The *they* referred to in this verse are precisely the people who have just been set free by the Anointed One. The restored ones, in turn, become the agents of restoration in the city. The ruins of people and communities lie all around us. Generations who have grown up never knowing anything of God's love are with us every day, at work, school, university and the coffee shop. These dear ones have been brought up feeding on the lies which come from the father of lies, Satan, since their earliest years. These are the people outside of church, but many of us also know of church congregations torn apart by division, whilst the scattered precious believers have given up on church because it all became too painful. The devil is a wrecker, but the kingly anointing is apostolic – for building. Paul the apostle described his ministry as that of a master builder laying a good foundation:

> *According to the grace of God given to me, like a skilled master builder I laid a foundation, and someone else is building upon it. Let each one take care how he builds upon it. For no one can lay a foundation other than that which is laid, which is Jesus Christ.* (1 Corinthians 3:10,11)

When we are clothed in the kingly anointing we know our daddy's rich and our mama's good looking. We come into desolate situations as a reservoir of hope. We bring heaven's resources to break up the stranglehold of poverty. It's exciting to see just how confident Jesus was in the anointing he had given to his disciples – they had become concerned for the crowds who had been with them for a couple of days and were hungry. Jesus' team naturally assumed this must be the time to wrap up the revival and send the multitudes home. Jesus, as usual, had a far more provocative solution: 'You feed them.' At this point, I doubt if any one of the disciples was thinking, 'It's OK, fellas, I've got this; my daddy's rich.' The only resources they could see was a boy's packed lunch – what they couldn't see was the kingly anointing all over Jesus. In God's order kings create a culture of provision and prosperity – just check out Solomon. In the face of their bewilderment and sense of inadequacy, Jesus blessed the food, broke it and handed it to the disciples to distribute it. As they handed it out to the people seated on the grass, the miracle happened: bread and fish multiplied in their hands.

Jesus wants us to feel the miracle happening in our hands.

When we're not especially feeling it

Today I am in Merida, a city in Venezuela. Venezuela has suffered immensely in recent years from insane levels of inflation. The economy is officially down the toilet, leaving chronic shortages of basic daily necessities such as shampoo, deodorant and water. Food is expensive and businesses are failing. This once exuberant, colourful nation has followed the downward spiral of Zimbabwe with people forced to eat from the garbage and steal from each other. Caracas has recently climbed to the top of the league of the most dangerous cities to visit. I am here with my friend Clive, my brother, his Venezuelan wife and their eldest son. We are ministering to the church in Merida and to pastors and leaders from across the state. Too many of them tell stories of being held at gunpoint whilst their home is robbed, others of family members shot dead as burglary turns lethal.

My own problems seem so minor in comparison, but recently I have been plagued by parts of my face swelling at random to maybe three times their normal size. It has usually been one or the other side of my mouth and adjacent cheek or one of my lips – each time it has taken days to return to normal. The doctors are puzzled and have taken blood tests which show that I am not allergic to any of the usual suspects. The other confusing thing is that the swellings have usually started in the early morning, about 5.00 a.m., before I have eaten anything. Anyway, yesterday I had preached and the Holy Spirit was moving; the time praying for people afterwards was really good, but then, just as we left for lunch, I felt the tale-tell tingle in my right cheek. The swelling typically happens really quickly – a few minutes – but I have found that with a powerful dose of antihistamine the moment I feel the first signs I can stop it becoming too extreme. Even so, as we arrived at the home of the kind people giving us lunch, I already looked like a weird caricature of me. I tried to be normal and enjoy the hospitality, but I really just wanted to go home to England and hide away with my family. In the obligatory group photos after lunch I tried to cover half of my face with my hand.

In the night I became aware of the other side of my face swelling, and looking in the bathroom mirror, I saw someone from the *Planet of the Apes* looking blearily back at me. Joy! I lay in bed praying, with the urge to hide away growing stronger by the moment. It was Sunday morning and I would be expected to be at the church service, although Clive was due to preach. I didn't feel much like an anointed king, or someone with any spiritual authority at all. Then at 6.30 a.m. I sensed the Holy Spirit begin to whisper in my heart, so I made a note on my phone: 'I desire to release the miraculous through you. You have come to the end of your own resources which is where I need you to be. I am releasing healing and joy.' As I finished writing this and a couple more sentences, I wrote the heading *Merida* and the date above it. In that moment I realised that this was not only an encouraging word for me, but a message for the people of the church in Merida. So, I pulled up my big-boy pants and went to the meeting, in spite of the comedy face. I told of my cheek-inflating experiences and read out the short message. Everyone cheered. Clive went on to give a great preach, and as we prayed for people to receive the Holy Spirit, God was moving powerfully. In this time, my brother and I prayed for a young woman with learning disabilities whose arm was immobile and useless having been damaged in an accident. We simply commanded it to be restored in the name of Jesus – instantly she began to wave a now fully mobile arm around her head. So cool! In a few hours God had confirmed his word both to me and to the church.

(That night, in the early hours of the morning, my tongue swelled up until it was too large to fit in my mouth and I had to breathe through my nose . . . but that's another story!)

The Queen probably has days where she just feels bored, or hungry, or just not very queenly, but she is still the anointed monarch – everyone around her knows that. Here is the point: it's not us doing the miracle, it never is, even when we feel like a million dollars – it is the one who has Christed us who does the impossible. This means it does not matter how I'm feeling today. Today I may be feeling particularly super-ace, or maybe nauseous, or maybe just normal, but as Peter asked, 'Why do you stare at us . . .?'

Blooming desert

On a trip to Central Asia, two friends and I spent the night in the desert. When we left the city in the ancient Lada Niva with our Russian guide, Ivan, it was very hot. After hours of driving and a break to replace a wheel, we stopped in the middle of nowhere. We set about putting up the tents in a barren landscape, starved of moisture, dotted with the remains of scrubby bushes devoid of any signs of life. As we finished, the sky rapidly darkened, the temperature plummeted and a swirling sandstorm rushed though. The roar of the wind, the stinging sand in our faces, brought in its wake rain – what were the chances? The storm subsided and Ivan (no speaky English) cooked us lamb and fish kebabs on a fire. Delicious, apart from the light dusting of sand. The desert night returned to still-ness all around us. Not a sound – no distant drone of traffic, no TV, no phone. Total silence – nothing between us and an endless black sky dense with twinkling lights reaching us from zillions of miles away. We spent the night warmed by a huge flaming crater in the ground where a subterranean gas reserve has silently burned like a furnace for over sixty years. As we drove back to the city the next morning, we saw the miracle – the brown sand of the desert had become pink with thousands of tiny blooms. That small (by English standards) drop of rain had made the desert burst into blossom overnight.

The kingly anointing is upon us to bring rain to spiritual deserts. Because of the anointing, we actually shift the status quo; we change the spiritual climate. 'A king's rage is like the roar of a lion, but his favour is like dew on the grass' (Proverbs 19:12 NIV). Where there is no sense of the Holy Spirit everything feels like a desert, dry as a bone. When someone brings the kingly anointing – the favour of God – it is like the dew; fresh, revi-talising and such a relief! Moses describes perfectly, the kingly anointing on a preacher: 'May my teaching drop as the rain, my speech distil as the dew, like gentle rain upon the tender grass, and like showers upon the herb' (Deuteronomy 32:2).

Please, God, give us anointed preachers!

Justice

One thing which seems to be indelibly coded into the DNA of human beings is a powerful sense of justice. The smallest of children soon start protesting to their parents that it isn't fair. Who even told them that fairness is a thing? Our innate sense of justice is one of God's own characteristics; it is one of the indicators that we are created in his image. 'He loves righteousness and justice; the earth is full of the steadfast love of the Lord' (Psalm 33:5). Establishing justice and righteousness are key elements of the kingly mandate which God brings about through his anointing. Speaking prophetically of Jesus, Ethan the psalm writer declares, 'Righteousness and justice are the foundation of your throne; steadfast love and faithfulness go before you' (Psalm 89:14).

Justice breaks up the controlling monopoly of the corrupt and lifts up those who are poor and oppressed. Look at these beautiful lines from Psalm 146 – see how they powerfully echo the words of Isaiah 61:

> *Who executes justice for the oppressed,*
> *who gives food to the hungry.*
> *The Lord sets the prisoners free;*
> *the Lord opens the eyes of the blind.*
> *The Lord lifts up those who are bowed down;*
> *the Lord loves the righteous.*
> *The Lord watches over the sojourners;*
> *he upholds the widow and the fatherless,*
> *but the way of the wicked he brings to ruin.* (Psalm 146:7–9)

All around the world, Christed ones are operating in their kingly authority by feeding the homeless, rescuing children from prostitution and young women from sex trafficking, and bringing radical change in countless other areas where injustice has reigned. Brian and Margaret Burton in Thailand tell the most extraordinary stories of how the kingdom of heaven is advancing in power and breaking down the stranglehold of corruption, even at the highest levels of government in this Buddhist nation. It is also true, of course, that many great works tackling gross injustice are being undertaken by people who do not follow Jesus, even some who may consider themselves atheists. In reality, however, even these are actually responding to the kingly rule of Jesus and are assisting in his agenda unawares.

In the prophetic passage from Isaiah, often read at Christmas, the prophet describes the reign of the Messiah: 'Of the *increase* of his government and of peace *there will be no end*' (Isaiah 9:7, emphasis added). He does not just characterise the reign of the Messiah as bringing peace, but tells how its influence is constantly increasing and expanding for ever. This is echoed by the interpretation of the dream of Nebuchadnezzar given by Daniel, which speaks of a kingdom which grows to fill the whole earth.

Isaiah also goes on to highlight how true followers of God are not just following a set of beliefs and rituals, but are engaged in God's business of rolling out justice in the community.

> *Is not this the fast that I choose:*
>   *to loose the bonds of wickedness,*
>   *to undo the straps of the yoke,*

to let the oppressed go free,
   and to break every yoke?
Is it not to share your bread with the hungry
   and bring the homeless poor into your house;
when you see the naked, to cover him,
   and not to hide yourself from your own flesh? (Isaiah 58:6,7)

This is precisely the work Jesus threw himself into. By coincidence, this evening I have just had the privilege of hearing John Kirkby, the founder of Christians Against Poverty sharing his story and his passion for the poor. He read the next few verses from this chapter in Isaiah from *The Message* version of the Bible. It was so powerful and graphically illustrates the heart behind Christians Against Poverty, but also the heart of God:

If you get rid of unfair practices,
   quit blaming victims,
   quit gossiping about other people's sins,
If you are generous with the hungry
   and start giving yourselves to the down-and-out,
Your lives will begin to glow in the darkness,
   your shadowed lives will be bathed in sunlight.
I will always show you where to go.
   I'll give you a full life in the emptiest of places –
   firm muscles, strong bones.
You'll be like a well-watered garden,
   a gurgling spring that never runs dry.
You'll use the old rubble of past lives to build anew,
   rebuild the foundations from out of your past.
You'll be known as those who can fix anything,
   restore old ruins, rebuild and renovate,
   make the community liveable again. (Isaiah 58:9–12 *The Message*)

Ballistics

Jesus also promised another kind of power from the person of the Holy Spirit: 'But you will receive power when the Holy Spirit has come upon you, and you will be my witnesses in Jerusalem and in all Judea and Samaria, and to the end of the earth' (Acts 1:8). The word the writer Luke used here for power is *dunamis* – it's easy to see the modern English words which come from this Greek origin: dynamo, dynamic and dynamite. In the New Testament it conveys a sense of the power or ability to get something done with an added supernatural dimension. Kingly authority, *exousia*, coupled with the X-factor *dunamis* of the Holy Spirit is like the authority of a uniformed police officer armed with the additional persuasive power of a gun.

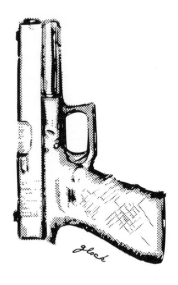

Here's another good Greek word to put in the mix and give it all a stir: *ekballo*. This is the word from which we derive English words such as ballistic, describing the incredible force which thrusts a missile into the air. It means to throw out with force, even an irresistible force. Jesus said, 'But if it is by the finger of God that I cast out (*ekballo*) demons, then the kingdom of God has come upon you' (Luke 11:20, parenthesis added). Jesus had enough authority and power in his little finger to fire demons out of people like a bullet from a gun and get a mute person talking again. My friend, who works as a therapist in a large mental hospital, was recently assigned a patient who was unable to speak. Bear in mind, as a health care professional, she is not permitted to mention Jesus or to offer to pray for the person she is there to help. During their first session the patient began to speak and was considered well enough to be discharged the next day. In the past six months she has seen numerous patients who suddenly recovered after their session with her and were sent home the next day. She is anointed to set the oppressed free. The Christing on her life is manifesting in acts of power – often catching her by surprise. She prays at home and in the car driving to work and the Holy Spirit liberates prisoners when she arrives.

Jesus demonstrated the authority of the kingdom of God by putting fireworks under the pants of demonic squatters who had been occupying human real estate until he, the Anointed One, showed up. In the previous chapter, we read that he appointed seventy-two people besides the Twelve, to send out into the towns and villages he was planning to visit himself. They were to be his advance teams, preparing communities for his arrival. This is absolutely fascinating. This group were not as personally close to Jesus as the Twelve – they had not received the daily close mentoring enjoyed by the apostles, but now were being sent out on the basis that people who received them were receiving Jesus (Luke 10:16). In chapters 8 and 9 of Luke we read some less than glamorous depictions of the Twelve – we see them bickering about who is the greatest, wanting to destroy a whole village by calling down fire from heaven and then failing to cast out a demon from a young boy. This is the Twelve, but then Jesus seems to add to his handicap by sending out seventy-two more who are even less qualified.

Evangelism #101

Before sending them all out, Jesus tells them that the harvest is vast, but that there are hardly any workers gathering it in. He is clearly not speaking about a harvest of wheat or barley, but people. He is talking about gathering the hearts of men, women and children and helping them reach a place where they are able to receive Jesus and so be reconciled to God the Father. 'Therefore pray earnestly to the Lord of the harvest to send out (*ekballo*) labourers into his harvest' (Luke 10:2, parenthesis added). This is not very British! Jesus is telling them to ask the Lord of the harvest – that's God – to put a firework under the pants of the labourers and shoot them out into the harvest. Jesus appears to be expecting the same reluctance from his labourers to get out of bed and go to work as he experienced from demons when it came to them having to leave their cosy human hosts. Not much has changed!

He makes the challenge even greater by saying to them, 'Go your way; behold, I am sending you out as lambs in the midst of wolves. Carry no money bag, no knapsack, no sandals' (Luke 10:3,4). He is, in effect sending these guys out into a dangerous situation – fluffy lambs into wolf neighbourhood, without any safety equipment, no risk assessment – not even a first aid kit. This is not a full-armour-of-God scenario – sword, shield, helmet, breastplate – he is sending them out barefoot. Shocking! What about the special shoes Paul talks about in Ephesians 6:15? We learn about this stuff in Sunday school! The task he gives them is not to explain the theology of why Jesus was going to die, or to preach a phenomenal sermon about God's love, in fact their first task is to simply give their peace to the house where they will lodge. (Ed Silvoso unpacks this strategy in his book, *Prayer Evangelism*.[5]) The second task is to eat whatever food their hosts provide. Nice. The third job was to heal anyone who was sick in the town. Now we can see why modern evangelistic programmes have become much more about explaining theology, because Jesus' method was scary! Jesus' method was demonstrate first, explain last. Although disciples today may be reluctant to head towards the harvest fields at all, most would be more comfortable talking about Jesus than they would attempting to demonstrate Jesus by publicly healing the sick in a community.

The explanation part was the fourth and last task of the seventy-two. Once the healings had taken place the preaching was easy, they could simply say that it was all done through the authority of Jesus, who happens to be the Messiah. When these unprepared, *ekballo*-ed missionaries returned, their stories were not about being savaged by wolves, or about feeling totally stupid, ill-equipped and unprepared, but rather that even demons obeyed them. They were in effect saying, 'You *ekballo*-ed us into the harvest and we *ekballo*-ed demons and sickness by acting under your authority.' Good job, everyone!

One more *ekballo* thought: God confronted Peter's racial prejudice and sent him to a house full of gentiles to release the anointing of the Holy Spirit onto them. God moved powerfully among the non-Jewish believers, clearly demonstrating that the good news was for them too. He even led Philip to a place where he could explain the good news to an Ethiopian government official. In spite of all this the church in Jerusalem became complacent and comfortable in its success. Peter even slipped back into his prejudiced ways and had to be confronted by Paul. Then came the horrific happenings in AD 70 which resulted in a huge scattering of Jews, many of whom were Christians, all around the world. This is now known as the Diaspora, which is actually an agricultural term meaning 'scattering seed'. No-one was praying for this to happen. Nobody wanted the Diaspora. This dark time turned out to be a major *ekballo* moment, resulting in a massive spread of the gospel into unreached areas of the world. We should beware of becoming too comfy – there is a lot of work yet to be done and the Lord of the harvest is still recruiting labourers from the ranks of the Cosy Club by the *ekballo* method.

I am an unashamed Charismatic, but it is worth a mention that the power of the Holy Spirit is not for decoration. It's not spiritual tinsel to make church services more pretty, but Jesus said, 'And you will be my witnesses in Jerusalem and in all Judea and Samaria, and to the end of the earth.' The *dunamis*, boom-shakka-shakka power of the Christing is to get the life-giving, oppression-busting, freedom-bringing life of Jesus into the whole world, starting right where we live.

Let's pause and reflect . . .

1. How much of your life is about getting through the day, keeping out of trouble and getting enough sleep to be able to survive tomorrow?

2. To what extent do you see the spiritual environment around you changing because of your Christing?

3. How much of your church life is about following a pattern that has been followed for a long time, which should not be interrupted on pain of death, or worse?

4. Could your ministry continue fairly well without words like *dunamis* and *ekballo* threatening to rock the boat?

5. Do you expect and go after supernatural manifestations of the Holy Spirit in your own life/in the life of your church?

6. What do you understand by the term, *exercising* your authority as a Christed one?

6: Craftsmen and Governors

Although the two main streams of anointing in the Bible seem to be kingly and priestly, the first example in the Bible of a person being referred to as 'filled with the Holy Spirit' is a guy called Bezalel. Bezalel shows up in the Exodus story mid-desert. The Israelites have successfully escaped from Egypt, crossed the Red Sea and survived the crash course in wilderness camping. They have become used to navigating by and responding to the presence of God as evidenced by the pillar of cloud or fire, depending on the time of day. Now God begins to instruct Moses to build a special tent as a focal point for the nation's interactions with God. The tent, known as the Tabernacle, was portable, but incredibly ornate. It was designed as an environment of worship and sacrifice. It was both the place where the altar of burnt offerings was sited, but also the altar of incense. It was also home to the Ark of the Covenant, the special box over which the brightness of the glory of God hovered. This Ark was made of beaten gold, adorned with two gold cherubim – I can't help wondering how the sculptor knew what cherubim looked like – and contained the stone slabs inscribed with the Ten Commandments, handwritten by God.

The LORD said to Moses, 'See, I have called by name Bezalel the son of Uri, son of Hur, of the tribe of Judah, and I have filled him with the Spirit of God, with ability and intelligence, with knowledge and all craftsmanship, to devise artistic designs, to work in gold, silver, and bronze, in cutting stones for setting, and in carving wood, to work in every craft. And behold, I have appointed with him Oholiab, the son of Ahisamach, of the tribe of Dan. And I have given to all able men ability, that they may make all that I have commanded you.' (Exodus 31:1–6)

The text goes on to list all the amazing areas of craftsmanship which were to be required in the execution of this extraordinary project, even down to the production of oil and incense. It seems most likely that these men, Bezalel and Oholiab, were formerly slaves in Egypt unless, perhaps, they were young men born in the wilderness. Whichever was the case, we might assume they had no knowledge or experience of craftsmanship, such as smelting gold, fine embroidery or perfumery, yet the Spirit of God *gave them ability*. Also notice that this anointing of the Spirit for craftsmanship fell on a whole bunch of other people too: 'And I have given to *all able men ability* that they may make all that I have commanded you.'

As the work on the Tabernacle began in earnest we read of *skilful women* who took on the spinning and weaving to make the priestly robes and the curtains, 'And every skilful woman spun with her hands, and they all brought what they had spun in blue and purple and scarlet yarns and fine twined linen. All the women whose hearts stirred them to use their skill spun the goats' hair' (Exodus 35:25–26).

From this account we learn two important things about the anointing of the Holy Spirit. Firstly that it is to do with God giving *ordinary* people *ability* (compare with chapter 2). The ability which comes from the anointing is supernatural. Secondly, as with the female spinners and weavers, it often involves the heart being moved, or stirred. The process of creativity requires movement. Something first begins to form inside us, before it becomes visible – it's like a gestation or pregnancy – the Spirit broods on us as at the moment when God began creation. Then our bodies move to carve, shape, weld or dance. The resulting work then has the power to move people when they see or hear the finished creation.

False start

As a painter and the son of a blacksmith, I love the fact that the first outpouring of the Holy Spirit on human beings that gets a proper mention in the Bible is to empower people to create beautiful things. The intricate work and the specialist knowledge required to create the items listed would naturally take centuries to acquire. It would have required knowledge such as is handed down through the generations, father to son, mother to daughter, master to apprentice, with successive craftspeople pushing forward the boundaries of what was possible. Turn the page in the Bible, though, and we read the tragic story of the golden calf. Whilst Moses was on the mountain receiving instructions from God about this extraordinary Tabernacle project, the people became bored and frustrated waiting for Moses to return. They complained to Aaron, Moses' brother and co-leader. He told them to bring items of Egyptian gold to him which he smelted to cast the image of a calf-idol from the molten gold, adding detailing by hand. Although Aaron came up with the bizarre excuse that the gold *just assumed the shape of a calf* when they melted it in the fire, considerable thought and artistry must have gone into its production. This is a classic piece of devilish hijacking. God is poised on the point of pouring out a creative spirit on a large number of people – he is even talking about it to Moses – but at the same time the devil tries to pre-empt God by inspiring the production of an idol through the same medium of creativity.

Reclaiming creativity

The devil has consistently tried to steal the creative realm from God's people. Now is the time for Christed individuals to respond to the creative Holy Spirit – to reclaim the visual arts, dance, design, literature, architecture and music along with high-tech digital design and innovation. Equally, we should not forget mathematics and science – these disciplines, not usually associated with the arts are arenas in which creativity and imagination can move the whole human race forward. There are divinely inspired breakthroughs waiting for those who will pursue God for the anointing of invention.

The writing of Zechariah gives us a tantalising peek at a prophetic scenario where God's people have been oppressed by certain nations, depicted here as horns. In the books of prophecy in the Bible, horns are usually seen as symbolic of strength, but the horn was also the container used to hold and pour out the oil used in anointing. We could say that these nations are empowered by a counterfeit anointing. The prophet then sees four *craftsmen* raised up as deliverers. (I like the New Living Translation, as it calls them blacksmiths!) 'These four horns – these nations – scattered and humbled Judah. Now these blacksmiths have come to terrify those nations and throw them down and destroy them' (Zechariah 1:21 NLT). I wonder what exactly the Spirit of God has in mind – what form that artisan-led deliverance looks like. I believe these deliverers are anointed agents of change. The craftsperson, or artisan, is actually a tough decision-maker. Everything he or she produces has been scrutinised by a creative eye; it has been subjected to a judgement based on a personal aesthetic. Watching an artist at work we see a constant process of appraisal – every mark is intentional and purposeful. My dad was so efficient with each hammer blow, not one was wasted. Each strike was perfectly weighted, exactly on target for maximum effect. Blacksmiths do not waste their fire. *Strike while the iron's hot*, is blacksmith talk. The yellow/orange heat of the iron is so valuable, optimising the power of his arm. This is so like the working of God – he does not waste any time or any process in shaping our hearts.

God's handiwork

We should not be sur-
prised to find that in the
Christing there might be
access to a whole new
realm of creativity, as
we read that 'All things
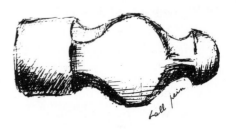
were made through him (Jesus), and without him was not any thing made that was made' (John 1:3, parenthesis added). In the book of Proverbs, wisdom is personified – some believe this is a representation of Jesus:

I was there when He established the heavens . . .
. . . when He marked out the foundations of the earth.

Then I was a skilled craftsman at His side,
  and His delight day by day,
  rejoicing always in His presence.
I was rejoicing in His whole world,
  delighting together in the sons of men. (Proverbs 8:27–31 BSB)

What an awesome thought, the Father, Son and Holy Spirit getting excited and rejoicing over the creation of the first ever man and woman – how much more rejoicing they must do over the new creation! 'Therefore, if anyone is in Christ, he is a new creation. The old has passed away; behold, the new has come' (2 Corinthians 5:17). Paul also writes to the Ephesians, 'For we are God's handiwork, created in Christ Jesus to do good works, which God prepared in advance for us to do' (Ephesians 2:10 NIV). God has created us all over again – you and I are the work of his creative genius – in Jesus, the Anointed One, in order that we get to go around doing more great handiwork which God has already done the preparatory work for.

We know that God does not live in buildings made by human hands – he said so himself – yet Jesus was not too grand to have an animals' manger as his first earthly bed experience, and apparently spent more than a few nights sleeping under the stars. Nonetheless, he does delight in creation and the creative process. When he pours his own creative Spirit into people, they, in turn, reflect his nature which is constantly creating, renewing and innovating. For example, the sky – the backdrop against which the human drama unfolds day by day, minute by minute. Without repetition or duplication, God continuously refreshes the screen we look at with infinite variety. Sometimes God's vast abstract canvas is so dramatic that it forcibly demands our attention, yet often more muted and in the background, as our gaze becomes fully absorbed in our own minuscule soap operas.

Vulnerability

Everything new seems strange initially. The creative person must, by definition, be pushing out alone into uncharted waters. Innovation, invention and works of art all involve taking big risks and making ourselves vulnerable to both criticism and rejection. The anointing of the Holy Spirit is the Spirit of Sonship – we will explore this in more detail in chapter 9. However, if we know that our dad is in the boardroom cheering us on as we make our pitch to the directors of the company, we will be way more bold and courageous, knowing we have his approval even before we start.

As parents, Anna and I have tried to foster any glimmer of creativity we have seen in any one of our four children. It is a great adventure. We have praised anything which has involved our precious ones pouring a drop of their own private heart out for the eyes or ears of another person. We have been the most uncritical and appreciative audience for everything from plays, puppet shows and homemade smoothies through to crazy interpretive dance. We have turned a blind eye to the hands of the clock moving way past bedtime as our junior Monet goes with the creative flow, and a deaf ear to the early efforts on the violin. Surely our Father in heaven is so much more excited as he watches his kids pour out our inner-selves in creativity.

Exile

Jump back in time a couple of millennia and a bit more. It was a terrible day, the day the Babylonians arrived in Jerusalem. After a miserable siege, the city finally fell: the gates burst open before a merciless surge of faceless foreigners, pouring in like a raging torrent through a broken dam. Everything with any value was ripped from its place. Family heirlooms, life savings, even the holy treasures from the Temple were snatched up as plunder – handcrafted sacred golden vessels devoted to the worship of the Living God taken as trophies to adorn the table of King Nebuchadnezzar. Along with these priceless artefacts and other trophies of war, were boys kidnapped from aristocratic families and the royal courts. Physically fit, good looking and of the highest intelligence, these young men were taken to add to the finest brains in Babylon to become part of the intellectual elite of what was the superpower of the day.

These young men, snatched away as their mothers and sisters were raped and their fathers killed, were then taken on an arduous journey on foot lasting many days. They arrived at their destination, dusty, terrified and at the point of exhaustion, were then shoved and herded by rough soldiers of incomprehensible tongue to be finally informed by an official that they were somehow the lucky ones. They were now to be treated as royalty; they would be dining on the finest food prepared for the table of the king himself. In return, they must study all the science, arts and religion of the Babylonian culture and become part of the court advising King Nebuchadnezzar.

And one more thing – they would be robbed of their manhood.

Survivor guilt, post-traumatic stress, probable castration and enforced assimilation into Babylonian ideology – quite a tough gig for these boys who had been on the fast track to the top jobs in Jerusalem. Daniel and his three friends were among those selected for this life. They were given new names; their own identities stolen and replaced with names associated with the gods of the Babylonians that the fine Jewish boys had been brought up to detest. Daniel's name became Belteshazzar, meaning 'Bel protect my life'. Bel was a Babylonian god.

The four friends made the decision to live as men of God and stay faithful to God even though to do this would mean putting their lives seriously at risk. For example, on one occasion Daniel's three amigos refused to bow down and worship a colossal image made of gold in the form of King Nebuchadnezzar at a massive public rally.[1] They were the only ones standing in a sea of prostrated humanity. This bold act of non-compliance became part of the process which led these young men to become top advisers in the Babylonian court.

Daniel was not a preacher, as we have mentioned earlier, he was not even a priest – in fact, he had been required to become an expert in astrology and divination.[2] This is the point where good pastors go into panic! What made Daniel different was that every single day, three times a day, Daniel intentionally stepped into the presence of God. These Babylonians had robbed him of his home, his family, his name and even his manhood, but they could not steal his relationship with God, unless he himself gave it up. Daniel and his friends were explicit from the very start that they would be more than willing to die, rather than relinquish their relationship with God.

Daniel had made it his unshakable habit to stand in the presence of God, in close proximity to the Anointed One, and, as a result, brought that anointing into his arena of work. He became known personally by the King as the most anointed man on his team of viziers.

> *At last Daniel came in before me – he who was named Belteshazzar after the name of my god, and in whom is the spirit of the holy gods – and I told him the dream, saying, 'O Belteshazzar, chief of the magicians, because I know that the spirit of the holy gods is in you and that no mystery is too difficult for you, tell me the visions of my dream that I saw and their interpretation.'* (Daniel 4:8,9)

> *This dream I, King Nebuchadnezzar, saw. And you, O Belteshazzar, tell me the interpretation, because all the wise men of my kingdom are not able to make known to me the interpretation, but you are able, for the spirit of the holy gods is in you.* (Daniel 4:18)

This is so cool! The pagan king believes in Daniel, the eunuch, because he can see the anointing of the Holy Spirit in him: *but you are able, for the spirit of the holy gods is in you.* In his lifetime Daniel serves under three or four different pagan monarchs. He becomes the chief vizier in the nation. He becomes fluent in at least three languages.[3] When he is in his eighties he is thrown alive into a pit of lions, where he spends a peaceful, but probably smelly night. Two of the four rulers become believers in God – and introduce Daniel's God to the whole nation – because Daniel has learned the secret of living in the anointing and bringing it into his work environment.

Government

Throughout the Bible we see many examples of people leading people and nations under the influence of the Spirit of God – governing under the anointing. Joseph has a difficult start and more than a few major setbacks, but ultimately becomes the governor of Egypt. He is the architect of a major feeding programme which saves the entire nation of Egypt from starvation, and in the process rescues his brothers, the famous Patriarchs of the nation of Israel, from being wiped out by famine along with their children and livestock.[4] Nehemiah, a civil servant working for a pagan king, receives the anointing of the Holy Spirit to rebuild the ruined wall of Jerusalem. He takes on disillusioned locals as his workforce, defies the opposition of hostile neighbouring people groups and completes the work in double-quick time.

The Holy Spirit has what it takes to enable us to run a small business, lead a multinational corporation or govern a nation. His business is not just to help preachers and worship leaders. The anointing is given to bring the kingdom of heaven into every dimension of human life.

The Spirit of the LORD will rest on him –
   the Spirit of wisdom and of understanding,
   the Spirit of counsel and of might,
   the Spirit of the knowledge and fear of the LORD –
and he will delight in the fear of the LORD.
He will not judge by what he sees with his eyes,
   or decide by what he hears with his ears;
but with righteousness he will judge the needy,
   with justice he will give decisions for the poor of the earth.
(Isaiah 11:2–4 NIV)

This Christing is available for politicians, mountain rescue teams, high court judges, football managers, headteachers, detectives, human resources departments, social workers, parents . . .

The non-religious specialist

One of Jesus' famous stories told how a man, presumably a Jew, had to make a perilous journey from Jerusalem to Jericho. To all of those listening to Jesus, this road was a well-known crime hotspot – the haunt of highway robbers. The poor chap was passing through the danger zone when he was attacked, beaten severely, robbed and left for dead. Jesus then told how first a priest and then a Levite also happened to be walking that way and discovered the badly injured man. In turn, both the priest and then the Levite saw him, but deliberately crossed over and walked by on the far side of the road. A little later a Samaritan came along. The Samaritans were the people the Jews loved to hate – yep, God's special people shamelessly indulged in institutional racism towards the Samaritans. Jesus then turned the story onto his Jewish listeners – the hated Samaritan took care of this victim of crime, giving first aid and then going to the trouble of transporting him to an inn and paying for his ongoing care.

The priest and the Levite were both religious specialists. They each earned their living by serving God as a full-time occupation. The priest was God's anointed representative for the people – people just like the injured guy. He was anointed for the purpose of helping people, but when the opportunity came to help someone in genuine need he made a mental excuse (I have found Christians particularly good at coming up with a 'biblical' excuse why *not* to engage with someone in need) and hurried on by. Likewise, the Levite who worked at the Temple in a practical serving capacity, found some convenient excuse and walked on by. Both of these men were called by God, anointed and appointed to serve the people, but blatantly did not in this case. The Samaritan, on the other hand, was presumably some kind of businessman, but he was the one who brought the anointing to the man in need. He applied oil and wine to the man's wounds. Oil and wine are both biblical metaphors for the Holy Spirit.

Cafeteria or boardroom

This is a powerful picture: the non-religious specialist, the secular businessperson, has gone to work prepared, making sure they are stocked up with the Christing of the Holy Spirit. They are then equipped to bring that anointing into any situation of need they encounter, whether it be in the work cafeteria or the boardroom. The non-religious specialist rubs shoulders every day with people just doing their thing – going to work, doing the shopping and buying coffee. Francis Chan describes how remote his life became from presenting Jesus to non-church people the more successful he became as a pastor. This led him to quit the church he had planted and helped to become successful and big in order to reconnect with the people whose feet never crossed the threshold of his building.

Let's pause and reflect . . .

1. What do you make of Pablo Picasso's famous statement that every child is born an artist?
2. Have you disqualified yourself from the ranks of the so-called 'creatives'?
3. Where does your creativity lie?
   - baking
   - motorbike customisation
   - football coaching
   - gymnastics
   - calligraphy
   - negotiation
   - What then ....?
4. Do you need to repent of refusing to believe that your creative spark could be part of God's strategy to bring his kingdom into your city? If so, here's a good prayer:

Lord Jesus, I repent and change my heart and mind about my creative gifts. I ask your forgiveness for belittling my own accomplishments, for comparing my skills negatively to people around me, on Instagram, or wherever. Today, I thank you for this gift of ...., I recognise that it came from you and reflects your heart. Today I declare it holy, set apart for you. I devote this gift of .... to your service. Let the anointing of creativity be all over me! From this day, I am expecting innovative ideas, fresh inspiration, good contacts, promotion and the ability to focus. Thank you – I love you, Jesus!

5. How much do you leave the job of reaching the lost souls you meet every day to some mythical expert who you imagine will do a much better job than you?

6. How will you respond when your boss asks to see you and offers you promotion?

7: All Flesh

And it shall come to pass afterward, that I will pour out my Spirit on all flesh; your sons and your daughters shall prophesy, your old men shall dream dreams, and your young men shall see visions. (Joel 2:28)

All means *all*

I'm getting excited again! Look at this language – *all flesh*. This is super-inclusive. Bear in mind, this is the Old Testament. This prophecy came at a time when the people of Judah had developed a very unique identity, separate even from the Northern Kingdom of Israel. They were very *exclusive*. As we have already discussed, from the days of Moses, God had been coaching them in how to be a Holy Nation (Exodus 19:6), set apart as his special people. However, as God speaks through Joel, the prophet sees a time in the future where not just the people of Judah are going to receive this, but men and women, sons and daughters, young and old, male and female servants – they are all going to get it! This is a super-widespread, super-indiscriminate outpouring of the Holy Spirit. When Joel prophesies this he doesn't put any preconditions on who the Spirit will come to – 'all flesh' seems to suggest *all flesh*. This is surely a challenging idea for most evangelicals.[1]

When the Holy Spirit comes rushing onto the 120 disciples on the day of Pentecost, Peter is quick to claim this section of Joel's prophecy, telling the crowds that this outpouring they can see before them is part of what Joel foretold all those years ago: 'But this is that . . .' (KJV). He takes what was happening in a very localised spot of the world – one room with overspill – and puts it into a global context. He says, in effect, that what you can see happening today is the visible tip of the proverbial iceberg; this is the outpouring of the Holy Spirit on all flesh. He does then go on to make the promise conditional on receiving Jesus and being baptised: 'And Peter said to them, "Repent and be baptised every one of you in the name of Jesus Christ for the forgiveness of your sins, and *you will receive the gift of the Holy Spirit. For the promise is for you and for your children and for all who are far off,* everyone whom the Lord our God calls to himself"' (Acts 2:38,39, emphasis added). Of course, everyone needs to receive Jesus, but sometimes we limit God in terms of in which order he is supposed to do things. God's theology is not always systematic to our way of thinking.

When Jesus gave the disciples the heads up about the Holy Spirit he did say, 'And I will ask the Father, and he will give you another Helper, to be with you for ever, even the Spirit of truth, *whom the world cannot receive,* because it neither sees him nor knows him. You know him, for he dwells with you and will be in you' (John 14:16,17, emphasis added). Jesus promised that the Holy Spirit they had become used to *dwelling with them* in the form of Jesus would come to be living in them. I guess they knew that their friend and rabbi, Jesus, was inhabited by the Holy Spirit and they had grown to know and love his presence. In this passage he clearly indicates that the world – those who have not yet received Jesus – cannot receive the Holy Spirit.

Well, certainly not in the way he describes for his disciples.
Let's hold that thought . . .

The main event

I grew up in a church culture that rarely mentioned the Holy
Spirit. He seemed to me like the spare part of the Trinity –
an afterthought tagged on to the Father and the Son. At the
Church of England school I attended as a young child, when
he was mentioned in the Grace, he was referred to as *the Holy
Ghost*, which made him sound even more remote and a bit
spooky. As I grew and began to understand more of the teaching in church, his role seemed restricted to bringing conviction
of sin; leading people to be saved. Of course, Jesus did say that
the Holy Spirit would do that and it's super-important, but he
is so much more. Let's take another look at Peter's early preaching. At Pentecost, he preaches as if the outpouring of the Holy
Spirit was the crowning achievement of Jesus:

> *This Jesus God raised up, and of that we are all witnesses. Being there-
> fore exalted at the right hand of God, and having received from the
> Father the promise of the Holy Spirit, he has poured out this that you
> yourselves are seeing and hearing.* (Acts 2:32,33)

and, as we have mentioned already,

> *For the promise is for you and for your children and for all who are
> far off, everyone whom the Lord our God calls to himself.* (Acts 2:39)

Peter teaches the crowd that Jesus lived this perfect life on earth,
was crucified and buried, but that his body did not begin to
decompose as one might expect. He tells them that God raised

Jesus up and took him back into heaven, to the right hand of God. This is particularly amazing, and should be a whole book, but let's try to unpack it. Before the Son left heaven to come to earth (to be conceived in the womb of Mary) he was God, not a man. He fully became a man, yet remained fully God. Now the risen Jesus, *a resurrected man*, has returned. This is not only amazing, it is such a victory – an actual bona-fide member of the human race has defeated sin, death and Satan. Jesus succeeded where Adam failed. Jesus became fully human, was then anointed with the Holy Spirit, and in the power of the Holy Spirit lived a sinless (but human) life. When the Father took Jesus back to heaven, Jesus received the authorisation to send the Holy Spirit as a gift to the earth to be *poured out* on human flesh.

It is interesting to note that John the Baptiser said that *Jesus* would baptise in the Holy Spirit and with fire, whilst Peter talks of the Holy Spirit as the *promise of the Father*. More on this later.

This is a master stroke. Jesus, phenomenal though he was (and is), could only be in one place at a time. He travelled around on foot and was very limited by the usual constraints of a human body. We get it – it's the same for us. The Holy Spirit, however, is a wind, the breath of God. In both Hebrew and Greek his name translates into breath, gasp or wind.[2] The whole human race alive today breathes the same air which is part of the earth's atmosphere. Likewise, the breath of God can affect and fill countless multitudes of people at the same time. The Holy Spirit is limitless, as is God. He will never be used up; God's supply of his anointing is inexhaustible. The Holy Spirit is the omnipresent, omnipotent, omniscient God – everywhere at once, all-powerful and all-knowing.

Yeasty

In the Jewish family everyone understood about leaven. It is a natural yeast used in baking to make the dough ferment. This fermentation creates little bubbles of carbon dioxide gas, which makes the bread rise, and produces alcohol which gives the irresistible freshly baked bread aroma. The baking of bread was a normal part of everyday Jewish family life. The regulations of the Passover feast, however, required totally unleavened flatbread to be eaten with the lamb. Jesus takes the idea of leaven and uses it as a metaphor for influence or teaching. He warns his disciples to beware of the leaven of the Sadducees and the Pharisees. These two groups represented the two main brands of Jewish religious thinking at the time. Jesus warns against them both. The former were very sceptical about spiritual things, but heavily into politics, whilst the latter were super-religious, controlling people down to the tiny details of life. Paul rebukes the Corinthian believers against a culture of bragging developing among the people: 'Your boasting is not good. Do you not know that a little leaven leavens the whole lump?' (1 Corinthians 5:6).

Jesus, on the other hand, also compares the kingdom of heaven to yeast. 'He told them still another parable: "The kingdom of heaven is like yeast that a woman took and mixed into about thirty kilograms of flour until it worked all through the dough"' (Matthew 13:33 NIV). I enjoy making bread – but thirty kilograms is a lot of flour to knead in one go, by hand! Anyway, this super muscular mama hid some yeast in this batch of dough, kneaded it all together and left it. The yeast got to work on the flour and the whole batch began to rise. The ratio of yeast to flour needed to make bread is roughly 8 grams per kilo. I make that 0.8 per cent. Not so much – yet what an effect. With no raising agent at all, you will end up making chapatis or tortillas. Perfectly good, but so different from the light airy bread with that deliciously fermented taste that is made with yeast. Here's the point: a relatively tiny amount of yeast affects a whole lot of dough – equally, a tiny amount of the kingdom of heaven has a massive influence on society. A few anointed people can transform a community, but also, one touch from God will begin to transform an individual's whole life. If we could create a spiritual version of thermal camera spectacles that enabled us to see just how much the leaven of the kingdom has affected people, we would be pleasantly surprised.

A couple of days ago I was talking to the owner of a cafe. He had asked me, 'Are you a born-again Christian, like?' (We were in Sunderland.) I was pleased that he could tell, just by talking to me. He then went on to tell me about a guy he used to share a house with who was also a Christian. It turned out that this young medical student had been an amazing advert for Jesus: 'textbook, like'. So my new friend already had some kingdom leaven working in him, then I was able to pray for him and bless his business, and he had a leaven level increase. In fact, the next day he told my friend that after I had prayed, he had had the best day for business in five years. Come on! It's starting to rise!

Encounter

It is said that a memory is always reinforced and made more memorable if it is accompanied by a feeling. The most powerful way for anyone to hear the good news about Jesus is in the context of an encounter with him. If the message of Jesus is brought as a piece of verbal information alone, albeit with a careful attention to detail, making sure all the information is correct, it may do the job – the person hearing the message may respond, but it is a bit like giving a dry crust of bread to a hungry beggar. Much better to give the guy a decent meal. Surely, if we can introduce Jesus in person, it must beat lengthy theological descriptions. As we read the gospels, again and again we see Jesus touching people and healing them before he preaches to them. Sometimes he seems to let them go without explaining anything!

I was talking to some teenagers about Jesus with a friend who is a vicar. The young people were enjoying some banter with us, but one of the girls was particularly interested. She began asking what it was like to be a Christian. My friend was trying to explain the steps to receiving Jesus, but she seemed to be answering a question this girl wasn't asking. I suddenly realised what this young person wanted to know: 'You want to know what it will feel like with Jesus in your life, don't you?' I asked. 'Yeah!' she replied. 'OK,' I said, 'I think God can stretch to a try before you buy! We will ask him to give you a taster.' We got her to stand up (her friends were sniggering now) and stretch out her hands as if she was going to receive something. 'Shut your eyes, so your friends don't put you off,' I said. We then prayed the simplest ever prayer: 'Lord, please let Laura feel your love and power right now.' She was silent a few seconds (her friends became silent too), then she burst out, 'Oh wow, I can feel it. He really loves me!' Then a few seconds later, 'Oh wow, he knows everything I've done – all the bad stuff – he's seen it all!' She started sobbing as the Holy Spirit brought her into the presence of Jesus: his amazing love, but also his complete knowledge of her, good and bad. It was so easy then to lead her through the prayer to receive him.

On one occasion I had the privilege of talking with a retired Sergeant Major from the British Army. He had served out his time and was now running a small haulage business as a civilian. He told me how his life had changed since coming out of the Army. The Army had given him a sense of identity and purpose. He had trained young men and they had become like his sons. He had held some of these young men as they died in his arms; wounded in combat. He had then gone in person to meet their grieving mothers, wives and girlfriends, to break the news to them and share in their pain. He described the day he left the service and had to return his uniform. He was smartly saluted on the way in, 'Morning, Sar'nt Major,' then as he handed over his kit the quartermaster responded, 'Thank you, Mr Jones.' That was it – all those years, all the honour of his rank gone in a moment. Me? I just listened to the story of a world I will never know. When he was done, I said, 'Can I pray for you?' He warned, 'You will be going where no man has ever gone before!' I put my arm round his big shoulders and prayed that the Holy Spirit would come and introduce him to Jesus. For a moment this warrior was silent. We both could sense the presence of Jesus all around us.

'Wow, thanks mate, I really felt that,' he said, eventually.

Many people who regularly pray for the sick, such as a friend who oversees Healing Rooms in the south-west of England, agree that we see more miracles of healing among people who are not yet believers in Jesus than among the church people.

A dear friend who worked for us in the church office came in to work one day with a heavy heart. Her brother-in-law had just received bad news. He had lost a lot of weight, so had been taken in to hospital only to discover that he had cancer of the pancreas and a very poor prognosis. He had been told to prepare to enjoy Easter with his grandson, but that he would be unlikely to make it to Christmas. I offered to travel down to his home with her to pray for him for healing. He accepted the offer of prayer. This was the first miracle, as he was an atheist. He was booked in for surgery at the hospital, but it was considered more of a formality than a realistic hope of bringing recovery. My friend and I made the two-hour journey to his home where we were warmly received. It seemed right that we should do our praying before enjoying lunch with him and his wife – after all, that was why we had come. I explained that I would be praying to Jesus, not sending positive thoughts to some life force, or similar. 'That's fine,' he replied with a big smile. Nice! We prayed, ate lunch and went home. A few days later, the surgeon operated and successfully removed a small thing the size of a walnut, contained in a discreet membrane. The hospital staff were elated. They called our guy the 'Miracle Man' and kept his walnut in a jar as a souvenir. He stopped being an atheist and received Jesus. He has gone on to live a full healthy life for years and has enjoyed multiple holidays with his grandson and the rest of his family.

One more cool story . . . One evening I had a call from a young woman whose mother, in her seventies, had collapsed while having a cigarette in her back garden. She had banged her head and had lost consciousness and stopped breathing for twenty minutes. The paramedics had been called who succeeded in getting her breathing again, but she was put into a medically induced coma as it was highly likely that she had sustained brain damage after that length of time without oxygen. When I received the call I was just about to sit down with Anna, my wife, eat some food and watch a movie. I had to drive twenty minutes to the hospital, so Anna and the movie would have to wait. On the way there, I was having a conversation with Jesus, which went, 'Lord, you and I both know that there is only one person in this car who can heal anyone, so . . . if anyone is getting healed tonight it will be because you did it!' I walked in to the Intensive Care Unit and at least eight of the woman's grown-up kids and partners were all in the waiting room looking pretty gloomy.

I recognised the girl who had called me and said, 'Hi.' I introduced myself to the group, at which point someone said, 'Are you going to do the Last Rites?' I didn't feel I should admit that I had no clue how to do the Last Rites, but said cheerfully, 'No, I've come to pray for your mother to be healed!' One of the family replied, 'She's not religious.' I answered that I didn't think her opinion particularly mattered either way at this point, as she was unconscious. I invited the family to join me round the bed and we held hands. Clearing my throat, I did my best prayer, but it seemed way  too short, so I did it again. 'That's it from me,' I said, 'it's over to Jesus now. Let me know when there is a change.' I left, not wanting to have to explain anything too complicated and risk sabotaging my faith. The next day the daughter texted me saying her mum had blinked her eyes a couple of times – 'That's good, I guess,' I said optimistically. She agreed.

The day after that, she texted me to say her mum had sat up in bed, pulled out the tubes and given the doctors her name and date of birth. A couple of weeks later we met in Asda. She is fine – no brain damage.

Jesus did it.

Going viral

Moses once said, 'Would that all the LORD's people were prophets, that the LORD would put his Spirit on them!' (Numbers 11:29). He was looking forward to a day when there would be a global outpouring of the Holy Spirit. What Moses wished for, Jesus made possible. This promise is *for all who are far off.* Imagine a whole community coming under the influence of the Holy Spirit – imagine a whole nation. Imagine a nation full of love, joy, peace, patience, kindness, goodness, gentleness, faithfulness and self-control – wow. Such a nation would have no need for law-enforcement agencies or law courts! Imagine the prosperity that would build up as married couples stayed together and brought up their kids; as employees quit stealing from work and taking bribes. Imagine the level of achievement in schools and universities as children and young people managed to learn in an atmosphere of respect and self-control. Imagine a national government where each one looked after not only their own interests, but also the interests of others.[3]

The Holy Spirit is a person. He is actually everything expressed in Jesus, and the Father in an omnipresent, invisible form. Everything Jesus loves, the Holy Spirit loves; everything the Father feels, the Holy Spirit feels; everything Jesus says, the Holy Spirit reveals to us. Jesus said, 'I will not leave you as orphans; *I will come to you*' (John 14:18, emphasis added). The difference between Jesus and the Holy Spirit is that Jesus could only be in one place at a time. The Holy Spirit could easily fill everyone alive on the earth at the same time. All the power God expressed in creation resides in the Holy Spirit (Genesis 1:2). The miracle-working power of Jesus is a manifestation of the Holy Spirit. When the Spirit of God comes into a human life, it is such an unequal relationship! It is like a skinny, nine-stone kid being jumped on by a seventeen-stone rugby prop-forward – although that is still a feeble comparison – the skinny kid then assumes the power and speed of the rugby guy.

The extremely cool thing is that God wants to do exactly that. He wants to pounce on frail, timid, fleshly humans and fill them with his amazing love, power and divine nature. He wants to live through those fleshly creatures and transform the rest of the world through them.[4] He is not in the least bit squeamish about our flesh – he has chosen it as a vehicle to display his glory. In fact, the writer to the Hebrews explicitly states that it is not angels that he helps (Hebrews 2:16), although maybe angels would mess up far less and would be more impressive. Jesus willingly became flesh. The anointing of the Christ was on human flesh.

Throughout history God has always chosen to give himself a disadvantage by working with and through weak, fleshly humans.

Let's pause and reflect . . .

1. How much of church has become a kind of historical re-enactment, with Pentecost, for example, as a stop on the church calendar but largely ignored the rest of the year?
2. Consider the little stories in this chapter; do you have stories of the yeast of the kingdom working through you?
3. Can you think why the outpouring of the Holy Spirit has not yet gone viral in your community?
4. Can you think of any historical examples (not in the Bible), where the Holy Spirit transformed a whole community?
5. Next time you find yourself sharing your faith with someone, be bold and offer to pray for them (there and then), with your hand on their shoulder. Welcome the Holy Spirit and watch what happens. Pray for whatever need they identified; if none, pray for a sense of God's love.

8: Weak Superheroes

Nobody special

Gideon was Mr Nobody-Special. He lived at a time in the history of Israel before they had a king. Israel was a motley collection of twelve tribes living in the 'Promised Land', pretty much doing whatever each person thought was a good idea. As a nation, they had gradually adopted the culture of the surrounding people groups and taken to worshipping idols. To wake them up to their sin, God allowed their neighbours, the Midianites, to oppress them. The pattern was that just when the Israelites had gathered in a decent harvest, raiding parties from Midian would appear and make off with the year's produce. The Bible says that the Midianites were as numerous as a plague of locusts. This was no fun at all.

On this particular day, Gideon is trying to escape detection from enemy spies on the lookout for an easy target, by threshing wheat inside a winepress. Suddenly, an angel from God appears, sits down under the tree nearby and begins speaking with him. 'The LORD is with you, O mighty man of valour' (Judges 6:12). This is funny, as he's hiding because he's afraid. In fact, if anyone is feeling like a warrior on this particular day, it is not Gideon. Gideon, however, doesn't find it funny at all, but asks the visitor why then, if God is with them, are they so badly oppressed by their enemies. Although his people had all the amazing stories in their past – stories of how God had miraculously brought the nation up from Egypt, it seemed that now, God had completely forsaken them and abandoned them to their enemies.

The angel chooses not to answer the question (it seems angels do this quite a bit), but continues to speak: 'And the LORD turned to him and said, "Go in this might of yours and save Israel from the hand of Midian; do not I send you?"' (Judges 6:14). This is still funny, because nothing seems to have changed – Gideon is still in the winepress, hiding in fear. Angels are great, because their reference point is heaven and God's awesomeness – they don't seem to factor in the human mindset at all! This statement from the angel makes no sense; we already know that Gideon has no natural strength, but now the angel says, 'Go in this *might of yours*' (emphasis added), or according to the NIV, 'Go in the strength you have.' We have always been taught to *not* act in our own strength, but here is the angel apparently telling Gideon to do just that. Verse 16 seems to be the clincher for Gideon, 'And the LORD said to him, "But I will be with you."' It reminds me of God's assurance to Moses in the burning bush saga (Exodus 3:12). At this point Gideon's attitude to his visitor changes. He asks him to wait whilst he goes into his house to prepare a gift of meat and flatbread. He kills a young goat, prepares the meat, makes a broth and uses over nine kilos of flour for his flatbread – this is a feast. Meanwhile, the angel waits. It must have taken Gideon at least two hours to make that meal, probably more, depending on whether the goat was to be medium rare or well done. Returning with the food he offers it to the angel. The angel instructs him to put the meat and bread on a nearby rock and pour the broth over it all. What happens next must have stayed with Gideon all of his life. The angel reaches out his staff, touches the food with the tip and, boom! Fire bursts out of the rock (there's the rock again) and consumes all of the food. At the same time, he vanishes, leaving Gideon alone. Gandalf moment!

The shocking realisation hits home: he has seen the angel of the Lord, face to face! Even more shocking is that he is still alive! In response to Gideon's terrified prayer, God speaks again, but not through the angel this time: 'Peace be to you . . . you shall not die' (Judges 6:23). That day, Gideon received revelation about the nature of God. His encounter with God inspired him to worship, so he built an altar, naming it, 'The LORD is Peace', *Jehovah Shalom*. Gideon's revelation becomes *our* revelation. In fact, other prophets like Isaiah, add to this revelation over the centuries and we learn that the Christ, the Anointed One, is indeed, the Prince of Peace.[1] That night God would speak to Gideon again, this time telling him to tear down his father's idol to Asherah and demolish the altar to Baal that stood on his father's property. Asherah and Baal both were Canaanite deities whose worship was associated with promiscuity and child sacrifice. Throughout Israel's history, the rituals associated with these two cults seemed to be a continual source of temptation to God's people.

The next morning, Gideon narrowly escaped a public lynching by the townspeople – who all turned out to be devout idol worshippers – when his dad stepped in. However, the part of the story which I am eager to get to is told in verse 34. All the Midianites and all the Amalekites and the people of the East all came together against Israel, they crossed the river Jordan and encamped at the Valley of Jezreel. It was the classic showdown: the massed hoards of the Canaanites versus the tiny demoralised huddle of Israelites. But then something happened: 'But the Spirit of the LORD clothed Gideon . . .' This was the game-changer.

Power dressing

Gideon still looked the same, still spoke the same, was still essentially the same guy, but was now clothed in an invisible God suit. A friend recently arrived at a leaders' meeting dressed in a smart suit, her make-up particularly sharp and her hair done – I commented that she looked great. 'Yes,' she replied, 'I had to have some tough conversations today!' She is a head-teacher and had to show some strong leadership that day, so had made a particular effort to dress for the occasion. She wanted to look professional and in control of the situation. Clothed in the Holy Spirit, Gideon was now dressed for the occasion. No matter how many men Gideon was to end up with in his army, the balance of power was now weighted conclusively in his favour.

After the resurrection, Jesus instructed his disciples to wait in Jerusalem 'until you are clothed with power from on high' (Luke 24:49). This clothing, or baptism in the Holy Spirit, is the game-changer for us. Anyone attempting to join the spiritual battle, which is normal life for the disciple of Jesus, is not dressed for the occasion without being clothed in power; clothed in the Holy Spirit – the Christing. When we are baptised as a follower of Jesus, we are baptised into Christ, the Anointed One – the one full of the Holy Spirit. Paul says, 'For all of you who were baptised into Christ have clothed yourselves with Christ' (Galatians 3:27 NIV). We are actually *clothed* in the oily Messiah at baptism. (I don't remember anyone telling me anything like that in preparation for my baptism.)

The enemy knows who you are

Reading on, we see how God cuts Gideon's army down from 22,000, to 10,000, then at the end of his Special Forces selection process Gideon is left with an army of 300 men. I want to say 'lol' at this point! This is crazy talk from a military perspective. The enemy are too numerous to count and Gideon has a grand total of 300. However, God is kind to his mighty warrior and wants to help him be brave, so takes him on a late-night walk into the enemy camp. I love God's humour: 'If you are afraid to attack, go down to the camp with your servant Purah' (Judges 7:10 NIV). God sent him down to the enemy to get encouraged! He sneaked into the camp with his trusty servant, under cover of darkness, and they listened outside a tent to the conversation going on inside. One guy had woken from a dream where a barley loaf had rolled down a hill into the camp and flattened the tent. His soldier buddy interpreted the dream: 'This can be nothing other than the sword of Gideon son of Joash, the Israelite. God has given the Midianites and the whole camp into his hands' (Judges 7:14). This is so cool, so supernatural and so God!

Gideon then knew for certain that God had given him the victory. But notice, the enemy knew who Gideon was better than Gideon knew himself. Our enemy knows who we are often better than we know ourselves. When we are clothed in the Holy Spirit, we are the devil's nightmare – the end of his control of a region.

Let's pause and reflect . . .

1. How do you regain courage when you feel overwhelmed by the challenges facing you?
2. How might you 'power dress' to tackle your 'Midianite army'?
3. Who do your family and friends think you are? Who do you think you are?
4. How does what you feel like on a particular day affect what risks you might take with God?

9: Properly Pickled

Proud Papa

pickled chilli

Back to Jesus' baptism. The heavens opened and the Father – God the Father – spoke over his Son, 'This is my beloved Son, with whom I am well pleased' (Matthew 3:17). It's worth a mention here that, as far as we know, Jesus had not yet preached any great sermons or healed anyone, he had yet to have his big showdown with the devil, and he had not turned any water into wine. He *had* done a phenomenal job of remaining sinless throughout adolescence and young adulthood, but this moment is about the Father publicly expressing sheer delight in his much-loved Son. We glimpse the passionate Father, unable to remain silent because of the love he has for his Son. In the same way, he gathered a sky full of angels to let rip with heavenly worship at the time of Jesus' birth.

This is God the Father. He is the one Jesus came to introduce to the people of the earth. Jesus pulled his Father beautifully into focus from the somewhat blurry and fragmented image we conjure up from reading the writers of the Old Testament. This is the Father who knows how many individual hairs we each have on our heads – who knows what we need even before we ask. This is the Father who paints the flowers and feeds the birds; the one who cares about the little helpless sparrow being sold at the market, dying of exhaustion. This is the Father of whom Jesus could say, 'If you've seen me, you've seen my dad' (my paraphrase).

Spirit of adoption

If we could say that Jesus was the visible expression of the Father in a human body for people to see, we could also say that the Holy Spirit is a tangible expression of the Father in a way which we can feel. We certainly cannot see him, but we can see and feel what he does. Jesus said, 'The wind blows where it wishes, and you hear its sound, but you do not know where it comes from or where it goes. So it is with everyone who is born of the Spirit' (John 3:8).

Today I am in Romania. Yesterday I watched as a sixteen-year-old boy knelt at the front of a church meeting to surrender his life to Jesus. He was an orphan. He had been looked after by a children's home for a while, then by another project where they found his behaviour too demanding, so gave him drugs to quieten him down. Eventually he was found living on the streets by a Christian volunteer from the UK who works on a project outside of the city. This guy reported having found the teenager to the police. The police asked him to take the young man into his own home as they had no other resources available. Thankfully, he was a good person to ask to do such a thing – he is honourable, compassionate and has another young man lodging with him. He then brought the boy to his church where he responded to the message of the good news.

Today, we prayed with this orphan-no-more, to receive the
Holy Spirit and to know that certainty of sonship which the
Holy Spirit alone is able to bring into our hearts. The apostle
Paul explains to the Roman believers that the Spirit they have
received from God is indeed the Spirit of Sonship, otherwise
translated as the *Spirit of Adoption*. Jesus was able to send the
Holy Spirit because he had completed the required legal trans-
action, paying the price for our adoption.

> *For all who are led by the Spirit of God are sons of God. For you did
> not receive the spirit of slavery to fall back into fear, but you have re-
> ceived the Spirit of adoption as sons, by whom we cry, "Abba! Father!"
> The Spirit himself bears witness with our spirit that we are children
> of God.* (Romans 8:14–16)

Adopting a child is an amazing act – it involves taking someone
else's child that they are unable to care and provide for, and
giving them a home. It means loving that child as if he or she
was your very own, even though you may not even be related
to him or her. It requires a choice that does not happen when
a couple naturally conceive. The Holy Spirit that God places
in us recognises God as our Father and reaches out to him.
The word *Abba* is an Aramaic close family term for father – it
has been likened to the English *daddy*. The Holy Spirit is the
one who makes the theology *feel* real. Ah, now we're heading
off into dodgy waters, because we're talking about feelings –
surely feelings are unreliable. Let's just look again at the scriptures. John, the special friend of Jesus, who called himself the
disciple Jesus loved, talks about the anointing. John was one
of the younger disciples – we read of him reclining with his
head resting on Jesus – he loved being especially close to Jesus.

He says that the anointing of the Holy Spirit is given to keep us
abiding – that is making our abode, or home – in Jesus:

> *But the anointing that you received from him abides in you, and*
> *you have no need that anyone should teach you. But as his anointing*
> *teaches you about everything, and is true, and is no lie – just as it has*
> *taught you, abide in him.* (1 John 2:27)

> *And by this we know that he abides in us, by the Spirit whom he has*
> *given us.* (1 John 3:24)

The Holy Spirit has been with the Father and Son as God since
literally for ever. This person, as we have said, *is* the anointing.
He has lived in unity with the Father since before anything was
created – of course he cries 'Abba'. He never wants to break
unity with the Father and the Son; he will never bless us walking away from intimacy with the Father. He keeps us abiding.

The Lost Son

Possibly the most famous of all of the parables of Jesus is the
story of the Lost Son. It captures the passion in the heart of
God the Father for his farthest-off children to return home. In
the story, Jesus tells of a man who had two sons. The youngest is impatient and wants to be free from the constraints of
home, quit working on the farm and to get out there and live
the dream. He comes to his father and demands that he split
his wealth between the two boys so that he can have his share
immediately. The father concedes – he must have sold land
and livestock to do it – but gives the younger son his share
of the estate. The son heads off into the sunset, embarks on a

spending spree – buying stuff and buying friends whilst partying until all the money is gone. His ultimate low point is reached when he finds a job looking after pigs. (Not a popular career choice among nice Jewish boys!) He has yet to be paid and has no money for food. He is so hungry, he even starts looking enviously at the pig food. Jesus says that at that point, he comes to his senses. He realises that his father's servants were living a much comfier lifestyle than he was – they had food and shelter. It made sense to head for home, to try to get hired by his dad as a servant. So he decides to pluck up courage, go back to his father, own up to his stinky attitude and ask for a job.

As the son approaches the family home, the father sees him while he is still a long way off. He gathers up his robes and, very undignified, runs to meet him. The boy begins his well-rehearsed speech, 'Father, I have sinned . . .' but the Father throws his arms around his neck and kisses him. This is fabulous! The King James Version puts it, 'But when he was yet a great way off, his father saw him, and had compassion, and ran, and *fell on his neck*, and kissed him' (Luke 15:20 KJV, emphasis mine).

We can read all kinds of extra stuff into this story from a modern psychological perspective, but we can be sure of a few things about this embrace. Firstly, the boy still smelled of pigs – he had not had time to wash. Secondly, when the father held him, he was still hungry. Thirdly, and most importantly, when he was in the father's embrace, he knew that now everything would change – he was still dressed in rags, but a servant had been sent to fetch the best robe; he had no money, but was about to wear his dad's signet ring; he had yet to eat, but the fatted calf was being prepared. When lost sons and daughters return to God the Father, he throws his arms around us whilst we still reek with the rank odour of our sin and folly. In that very moment, locked in the passionate embrace with our loving Father, we now have all that we need; everything is going to change.

Luke, who captured this classic, is also the writer of the book of Acts. He tells the story of the birth of the church, beginning with 120 fairly intimidated disciples meeting together after Jesus had returned to heaven. Jesus had instructed them to stay put in Jerusalem until he sent the Holy Spirit to them. He had told them that the Holy Spirit was going to be a great help to them and that it would be like him being with them personally. However, they had no clue what exactly to expect or how the Holy Spirit would come. When he did come the disciples were all together on the day of the feast of Pentecost. Luke describes a sound 'like a mighty rushing wind' which 'filled the entire house' (Acts 2:2). Flames of fire appeared on each of the disciples, they were all filled with the Holy Spirit and began speaking in tongues. In that moment they were massively changed; they burst out into the street, appearing to be drunk to the bemused people who had gathered for the feast.

Promise of the Father

Peter then addresses the crowd, explaining about Jesus sending the Holy Spirit, with a brand-new boldness. He calls the arrival of the Holy Spirit, the *promise of the Father*. Jesus had said, 'If you then, who are evil, know how to give good gifts to your children, how much more will the heavenly Father give the Holy Spirit to those who ask him!' (Luke 11:13). He was saying that the Father, who is absolutely, totally good; who would only give the most amazing gift ever; was more eager to give the gift of his Holy Spirit, than earthly parents who get a major kick out of giving good stuff to their children.

Three thousand people responded to his message and were baptised that day. This was Peter. What a phenomenal transformation of the guy who had denied all knowledge of Jesus the night he was arrested! Peter had been held in the Father's embrace. Now many lives were being transformed as he ushered others into that embrace.

Papa's embrace

Strong's definition of the Greek word used by Luke (transliterated: *epipíptō*), is 'to embrace (with affection) or seize (with more or less violence; literally or figuratively): fall into (on, upon) lie on, press upon.'[1] *Thayer's Greek Lexicon* uses the following terms: 'to fall upon'; 'to rush or press upon'; 'to lie upon one'; 'to fall into one's embrace'; 'to fall back upon'; 'to fall upon one'; 'i.e. to seize, take possession of'.[2] In Acts chapter 10, Luke uses this same word to describe the father's embrace in the story of the Lost Son as he does to describe the Holy Spirit coming both at Pentecost and at the house of Cornelius.

Luke also records the account of a young guy called Eutychus, who falls asleep whilst listening to the great apostle Paul preaching for hours. The problem was, he was sitting in a window and the room was upstairs. The young man is killed by the fall – a mean person might say he is bored to death by the preacher. Undeterred, Paul runs downstairs, throws (*epipíptō*) himself bodily on the boy and prays – boom! Eutychus returns to life; Paul carries on preaching! The point is, when the father embraced his returning son in the story, it was not a stiff British handshake, it was a full-on passionate embrace. Likewise, when the Holy Spirit came to the Gentiles in the house of Cornelius, the extravagant Father God came swiftly and forcibly in love to embrace this household: the first ever Gentile church. The outpouring of the Holy Spirit is a lavishly loving Father embracing his beloved children.

Many times in the Old Testament we hear of the Holy Spirit *rushing* onto people. The language describes something forceful; something which overwhelms the individual and transforms their lives. When Peter later recounts these amazing events to the other apostles at Jerusalem, he says, 'As I began to speak, the Holy Spirit fell on them *just as on us* at the beginning' (Acts 11:15, emphasis added). This was exactly the same experience as the 120 had received in the famous upper room in Jerusalem on the day of Pentecost. They had experienced the passionate embrace of Abba Father – the prodigal love of God falling upon them.

Overwhelmed and undone

In 1994 a businessman had taken my friend Clive and myself to Toronto to see the so-called 'revival' that was reported to be in full swing there. Our flight was diverted just before landing because there was a massive storm over the nearby city of Buffalo. I remember seeing the black clouds from the window of our plane and feeling a strong need to confess my sins to God, as I wondered if he had brought me to this place to judge me! I was not entirely convinced of how much grace God had left towards me at that time. I was not even sure, if God really was moving in Toronto, that I would get it – I was not sure it would work for me; maybe I would be the one God left out. By the third day of our visit, however, the three of us were becoming irresistibly affected by the Holy Spirit, in such a way that we felt increasingly drunk. It was intoxicating just being in the glorious atmosphere that was pervading the church at that time.

On the fourth day, after a night of being unable to sleep due to the intoxication of the Holy Spirit, we made a trip to Niagara Falls. There we saw another natural picture of what God was doing in the realm of the spirit. Millions of tons of water per second were pouring over the edge of the falls creating one of the most phenomenal spectacles on earth. The sheer power was overwhelming. Both the storm over Buffalo and Niagara Falls turned out to be powerful metaphors of what has been a most incredible outpouring of the Holy Spirit. Whole nations have been affected by individuals caught up in this glorious move of God. What happened to me later that evening was like stepping into a heavenly version of Niagara Falls made entirely of light and love. I was completely overwhelmed by the raw power of the love of God. It was impossible to remain standing for more than a second, I was finished – overcome. That evening I was undone by the sense of the Father's immeasurable love and kindness towards me – I have remained forever changed by the experience.

The Toronto people dubbed this move of God, 'The Father's Blessing'. We have come to understand since, that what happened to us was the Papa's embrace. He 'fell' on us just like he fell on the disciples in the upper room and at the house of Cornelius.

Pickled people

John the Baptist identifies Jesus as the one who would baptise
with the Holy Spirit and with fire. This is all very dramatic. The
New Testament Greek word translated 'baptise' also appears
in an ancient Greek recipe describing the process of pickling
vegetables. The item to be pickled is plunged into vinegar or
brine. The vegetable is left submerged, or baptised, in the pickling liquid for weeks or months. The result is a preserved food
item, which would normally be mouldy and perished after a
few days, now perfectly edible months later. The noticeable
thing about pickles is that their flavour changes – they all taste
of vinegar (or brine). In fact, pickled eggs even change texture
from being soft to become more rubbery. The acid in the vinegar changes the nature of the protein of the egg white.

The baptism that Jesus brings is not just a pleasantly peaceful
feeling which passes, or even a new-found ability to speak in
tongues; rather, it is a total immersion in the person of the
Holy Spirit. Jesus came to pickle people in the fiery divine
character of the Holy Spirit. The point is, this baptism is in a
person, not a thing, or a feeling. The anointing is what happens
when the living breathing person – the Holy Spirit – envelopes
and covers the fragile flesh of a human being. This is beyond
wonderful! This is truly awesome! Amazingly, this phenomenon is limited to human beings. However cool they are, angels
don't get to experience being baptised in the Holy Spirit or the
radical transformation brought about by what Peter describes
as becoming a partaker in the divine nature. 'And because of his
glory and excellence, he has given us great and precious promises. These are the promises that enable you to share his divine
nature and escape the world's corruption caused by human
desires' (2 Peter 1:4 NLT).

Did you see that? As we become pickled by the Holy Spirit and take on the divine nature – we start tasting like Jesus, and we escape the corruption caused by the world. Our natural environment carries all sorts of mould spores and bacteria which cause decomposition of food. Pickling protects food from being susceptible to this process; likewise, the presence of the Holy Spirit keeps us from being corrupted, broken down and decayed by the effect of the death and sin in our environment.

Let's pause and reflect . . .

1. How was your relationship with your earthly dad?
2. To what extent do you project that onto God the Father?
3. What behaviour might be displayed by an orphan who remained unsure of their new parents' love for him or for her?
4. Do you detect any tell-tale 'orphan' behaviour traits in your own relationship with God?
5. Here is a good prayer:

Holy Spirit, you are the Spirit of adoption, you come from the Perfect Father and the Perfect Son. Wrap me in Papa's passionate embrace. Forgive me for all the performance orientated behaviour I have indulged in, believing that I can earn your love. I surrender to your relentless pursuit of my heart. I forgive my natural father for the times he modelled a poor image of you, on which I have based my expectations of you. Please reveal to me day after day, not just in my head but deep in the core of my being, what it means to be a dearly beloved child of my Abba Father.

10: Sons of Fresh Oil

You are the light of the world. A city set on a hill cannot be hidden. Nor do people light a lamp and put it under a basket, but on a stand, and it gives light to all in the house. In the same way, let your light shine before others, so that they may see your good works and give glory to your Father who is in heaven. (Matthew 5:14–16)

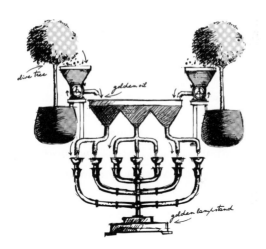

olive tree

golden oil

golden lampstand

Light of the world

In this famous statement, Jesus adopts a powerful image. Everyone is familiar with the need to see in the dark. In our modern homes we can just flick a switch and fill the room with light; Jesus' listeners had to light oil lamps. It is, however, the same basic deal – we can't see in the dark without some kind of artificial light. To extend Jesus' logic, we could say that if his disciples are the light of the world then without them, it follows that the world must be in darkness.

In John's gospel account, he records Jesus *himself* claiming to be the light of the world.[1] In the following chapter he expands this thought with, 'As long as I am in the world, I am the light of the world' (John 9:5). As if to illustrate this point, moments before, he had just healed a man who had been born blind. He had actually brought *light* into the eyes of a man who, until then had only ever experienced darkness. Nearly seven centuries before Jesus, Isaiah prophesied: 'The people who walked in darkness have seen a great light; those who dwelt in a land of deep darkness, on them has light shined' (Isaiah 9:2). Jesus then, appears on the world stage, opens blind eyes and claims to be this very light. He goes on to quickly point out that he is present as the light only for a season, then the job will fall to his disciples.

Isaiah also prophesied that the light would be not just for the Jewish people, but for the Gentiles also: 'It is too light a thing that you should be my servant to raise up the tribes of Jacob and to bring back the preserved of Israel; I will make you as a light for the nations, that my salvation may reach to the end of the earth' (Isaiah 49:6).

In Zechariah chapter 4, the prophet records a vision in which he sees an oil lampstand made entirely of solid gold, topped with a golden bowl full of olive oil. Around the bowl are seven lamps. On either side of the lampstand are two olive trees which seem to be supplying this golden oil direct to the lamps via two pipes. Zechariah then asks the angel standing next to him what these things mean. The angel then answers a question Zechariah has not asked, making the now famous statement, 'Not by might, nor by power, but by my Spirit, says the LORD of hosts' (Zechariah 4:6). He then goes on to say how Zerubbabel was going to finish the project he had started, the rebuilding of the Temple.

The prophet politely listens to the angel, but still has no clue as to the meaning of the olive trees and the lampstand, so he tries again:

> *Then I said to him, 'What are these two olive trees on the right and the left of the lampstand?' And a second time I answered and said to him, 'What are these two branches of the olive trees, which are beside the two golden pipes from which the golden oil is poured out?' He said to me, 'Do you not know what these are?' I said, 'No, my lord.' Then he said, 'These are the two anointed ones who stand by the Lord of the whole earth.'* (Zechariah 4:11–14)

This is a profound picture which initially sounds quite confusing. Let's try to break it down. The whole point of a lampstand is to give light. This particular one is powered by a supply of golden olive oil coming directly from two olive trees. The supply of oil is what is feeding the flame, giving light to the surrounding area.

According to the angel, this is a prophetic picture, depicting two 'anointed ones' who stand before God. The ESV footnote calls these guys 'two sons of new oil' which translates from the Hebrew, *yitshar*: fresh oil, and *ben*: son. This is so exciting! You will notice that there are two of these sons of fresh oil. If there was only one mentioned, we could maybe assume that this is a reference to the Anointed One, that is, Jesus – but there can only be one actual *Messiah*. (These two could, of course, be a reference to Joshua, son of Jehozadek, and Zerubabel, son of Shealtiel, who were key guys in the story.) But what if there are many sons – and daughters? In fact, Jesus brings 'many sons to glory' (Hebrews 2:10). These sons of fresh oil stand in the presence of the Lord of the whole earth and get anointed – smeared and saturated with the Holy Spirit – enabling them to supply the flow of oil which enables the lamp to keep burning. Hold that thought . . .

Foolish virgins

Jesus told many parables, that is, stories with a very obvious, accessible natural meaning, to make a more cryptic point about something spiritual. A well-known parable is the story of the ten young women whose job was to wait for a certain bridegroom to return from wherever he had gone, to claim his bride and crack on with the wedding feast. I guess this was a pretty familiar scenario to Jesus' Jewish audience, although a little obscure to 21st-century Westerners. The whole point of the story seems to be that although the bride and her companions were expecting him, the exact time of the bridegroom's return was known only to his father, according to custom. The ten young women were expected to be ready with their lamps burning to welcome the groom when he arrived. But it was getting late, there was no sign of his arrival and they all became drowsy and fell asleep.

At midnight they were awakened by a shout that the bridegroom had arrived. This was their big moment! The girls quickly fixed their hair, checked their mascara and attended to their lamps. Each of the lamps was just about to go out as the oil had burned up whilst they were asleep. Five of them had wisely brought spare oil, so were able to refill their lamps and be assembled at the doorway, ready to welcome the groom. The other five begged the girls who had brought spare to give them some of theirs, but were out of luck – it was now all taken.

Jesus told how they had to hurry to the oil seller to buy more. It seems pretty brutal, but the story ends with the girls returning to find that the groom has arrived and the wedding party has started without them. They tried to get in but were turned away by the bouncers on the door. The point Jesus was making was that we, like the girls, do not know when the bridegroom, that is, Jesus, will return: 'Watch therefore . . .'

Jesus equates the light of a lamp shining in the darkness to our lives representing God in the earth. We, his disciples, are the main signpost pointing people to the Father. In the present darkness and confusion of multiple religions competing with materialism and atheistic optimism – millions of different voices yelling their maxims and muttering their mantras – Jesus has given responsibility to his Christed ones to shine brightly, pointing out the way to the Father until he himself returns.

Back to the question Zechariah never asked, but the angel answered anyway: *How will we ever get this massive job done?* The very practical girl, Mary – soon to become the mother of Jesus – did ask the angel Gabriel the same kind of question, 'How can this be, as I am a virgin?' The angel answered Zechariah, 'Not by might, or by power, but by my Spirit says the Lord of Hosts.' The angel answered Mary, 'The Holy Spirit will come upon you, and the power of the Most High will overshadow you' (Luke 1:35).

Same answer: by the Holy Spirit.

God never calls us to do something we can already do by ourselves. When he calls us, we will always need miracles and his supernatural help. There is no way the task Jesus has set before us of making disciples of all nations is going to be done using our human resources alone.

We gonna need oil, baby!

If we are to be the light of the world and keep our lamps burning brightly until Jesus returns, we need to be staying topped up every day with the oil of the Holy Spirit. If our lights are going to shine and we are going to do the stuff Jesus did when he was

can of fresh oil

present as the Light of the World, we need to know how to stay oiled up. The wise virgins in the story directed their not-so-wise friends to the oil sellers to buy some. Zechariah, on the other hand, saw that there are oily people standing in the presence of God, whose job is to supply oil to keep the lamps shining. These people know how to stand close to Jesus, the Anointed One – the oil provider – and get filled up with the Holy Spirit. These anointed ones always seem to have enough to give away. When we start running dry, the smart thing to do is get to an oily person and ask them to share some oil with you by praying for a fresh impartation.

It is worth a mention here that listed among the foundational teachings found in Hebrews 6 is 'laying on of hands'. For the first-generation believers, the laying on of hands was normal practice, important enough to be considered foundational.

Foundations are laid first; everything subsequently built stands on those foundations. When Simon the Magician saw what happened when Peter and John laid their hands on people to receive the Holy Spirit, he was willing to pay good money for the gift he saw operating through the apostles (Acts 8:19). I would humbly suggest that he saw something more than people with nice peaceful expressions on their faces. I'm sure he saw the power of the Holy Spirit transforming people in real time, along with all kinds of outward manifestations.

Help or hazard?

In John's amazing vision, the book of Revelation, we see Jesus holding seven stars in his right hand and walking among the seven golden lampstands in heaven. The seven lampstands represent the seven churches that were then operating in the province of Asia, now known as Turkey. He addresses these churches and gives each of them a rebuke, an encouragement to press on, or a bit of both. In his remarks to the church in Ephesus, it seems to start well: 'I know your works, your toil and your patient endurance . . . I know you are enduring patiently' – words which could be applied to many churches in the 21st century. Then comes a rebuke: 'But I have this against you, that you have abandoned the *love you had at first*' (Revelation 2:2–4, emphasis added). Jesus tells the church to remember the heights from where they have fallen; he commands them to repent – change their hearts and minds and turn around their behaviour – and do the things they did at first.

Being commanded to repent is something we usually see as a remedy for sin – like reverting to a life of drug dealing, not falling out of love. The church at Ephesus had once loved Jesus with a fiery passion, but now they were just soldiering on, being patient and working hard. This church was not just any old church; the church in Ephesus had been planted by the apostle Paul; Timothy had been a leader there, as was the apostle John himself. This must have been a hard message for John to hear about his home church – Jesus is pretty tough with them – he tells them that if they don't repent, their lampstand will be removed. If a lamp is doing what it is made for, that is, giving light, it should be given a prominent place so that it can light the whole house. If the light has gone out, however, and the house is in darkness, a lampstand in the middle of the room has become a trip-hazard and may end up causing an accident if not removed.

A church which has lost its first love for Jesus is like a lamp which has run dry and has no oil and no flame. A church which does not light the way to the Father is a dangerous and confusing obstacle to those who are stumbling around in darkness. At Pentecost, the oil of the Holy Spirit came into the church, bringing a flame which rested on each of the disciples. This flame spread all over the known world: in a few short years it had turned the world upside down. By the time

of John's vision, it seems the flame in the church in Ephesus had begun to burn dangerously low.

Now, too, at our point in history, the Western church is also in great need of a trip to the oil sellers.

Let's pause and reflect . . .

1. Where is your light shining most brightly?
   - Under a basket
   - In church meetings
   - Everywhere you go
2. How can we 'buy oil' – what does that even mean?
3. Are you oily enough to be a resource of supply to others?
4. Is your church like a city on a hill which cannot be hidden, or an enclave in a bunker trying to avoid enemy fire?
5. What would happen if your church ceased trading – closed down and packed up tomorrow?

11: Oily Lovers

Anointed drum skin

Our son Josh began to learn the drums when he was about ten years old. In our ongoing attempt to encourage a creative (which seems also to mean, noisy and messy) atmosphere in our home, we bought him a drum kit. We did not have acres of room in our house, so for years the drum kit lived in his bedroom. Josh had talent and lessons, but like a lot of young musicians, did not always manage to find the motivation to practise. Then one morning he noticed oil on the skin of his snare drum, so came to find Anna and myself to show us this thing which had come to pass. Nothing else in the bedroom was oily and there was no sign of where the oil might have come from. We wiped the oil off the drum skin, but the next day it was back. This continued for a few days until we all assumed it was something to do with God. We asked Josh if he thought God was trying to get his attention and what he might be trying to say.

Josh responded instantly, 'I think God wants me to be a worship leader.' This declaration, however, did not result in the making of a child prodigy, but his mum and I did hide the word in our hearts. At the age of about sixteen Josh drifted away from God. He stopped coming to church with us. There was no big scene, just a quiet intentional shift. This experience with the drum skin, along with other prophetic words we had received about him, became ammunition that Anna and I fired back to God in prayer on Josh's behalf many times. He was still living in our home, but not as a follower of Jesus. About eight years later, approximately a year ago from the time I am writing, Josh had a break up with a girl he had begun to really love. We had never seen him so devastated. He sobbed and sobbed, clinging to us (he's a big muscular guy who towers over us), begging us to pray.

With no warning he began to pour out the most stunning prayer, returning his heart to Jesus. They were the words every pastor wants to hear when people turn to God – genuine heart-felt repentance, with tears. I could not have scripted it better if I had sat down and tried to write a good prayer for a returning prodigal. His life was transformed. Suddenly he was in church for every meeting, he was finishing work early to get time to speak to one or another of the younger pastors, he started working on our homeless project and, without us saying anything, he started practising the drums.

After nearly ten years of not even talking about playing drums, he started spending at least an hour every day in the shed practising. He now plays regularly as a member of the worship band. People have commented how he releases something unique and prophetic into the atmosphere of worship when he plays. The drum booth may not be the usual place to find a worship leader, but he has so clearly received an anointing from the Holy Spirit to bring God's people into a great place of encounter with God.

Which comes first?

Out on a remote hillside, looking after sheep, is not the place you would normally expect to find a king. However, this was precisely where you would have found the young man who was to go on to become Israel's finest ever king. Long before he was anointed monarch David was a worshipper. When he was a nobody – a simple shepherd boy – he had already learned a major secret. In fact, when God described him as a man after his own heart,[1] it was because David had already become exactly that. I'm sure David stumbled on the discovery that when he played his harp and sang certain songs, he felt a strange but lovely connection with God, so just kept doing it. The Old Covenant, which was the order of the day in the time of David, was all about sacrifice. It had no real provision for music as part of corporate worship. The instructions from God for the Tabernacle included the making of a number of silver trumpets. These were sounded to gather the people together and for giving the signal to move camp. They were also used in certain festivals, but there is no suggestion that they were regularly played for musical reasons. Even though both Moses and Miriam his sister were worshippers – we have some of their songs preserved – we do not read of musicians or singers involved in the activities around the Tabernacle of Moses.

The performance of a gifted musician can bring a tear to the eye, or a crowd to their feet. It is no secret that music moves the soul. Society has always placed a high value on the truly excellent in the field of the creative arts – on the list of the richest people in the world are performers like ex-Beatle, Sir Paul McCartney. There is an interesting discussion about the percentage of what we call talent, as opposed to the daily self-discipline of sheer hard work which is required to make a truly brilliant artist – be that musician, painter, writer, or even athlete. As a painter, I'm sure a huge part of what is called talent is the joy of early success which rewards our creative or athletic efforts, and fuels the motivation to practise when others have given up. I can still remember the praise from my friends and my parents when they saw my early drawings, which made me go for better. Whatever the actual percentage, there does seem to be a partnership required between the discovery of the original 'gift' and the development of that ability through practice and striving to be better, which usually takes many years before becoming world-class, or even just really good.

When a musician, who may actually be a long way short of world class, plays or leads worship under the anointing of the Holy Spirit, something very different happens than when someone simply plays well – it is transformational. The musician is no longer merely playing for an earthly audience, but heaven, too, begins to get involved. This glorious interaction between earth and heaven is what Jacob saw in his vision of the stairway, with angels ascending and descending. People around become drawn into this atmosphere and begin to respond to God and open their own hearts in worship. An excellent public speaker may have the power, through oratory and rhetoric, to move people and even persuade them, but a preacher who is clothed in the anointing of the Holy Spirit brings heaven into contact with earth. In that environment lives are changed forever. This preacher or worship leader may equally have spent years developing their art, but they have come to rely on the Holy Spirit and yield their performance to his influence, allowing him to saturate all they do. There is an art of partnership with the Holy Spirit which we must develop alongside our natural skills.

Commenting on the death of Aretha Franklin on BBC *Breakfast News*, one of the Sisters Sledge said that she opened her mouth to sing and heaven came out. She also said that this legendary woman gave herself entirely to the Holy Spirit. It's fascinating to hear what people say as they try to explain what the Holy Spirit does when such a person sings. Aretha Franklin clearly moved people regardless of their faith, including journalists who reported the sense that although they had no belief in God, nonetheless experienced heaven when she sang.

Preaching, too, should not be seen as merely verbally passing on information – even doing it well; rather, it is allowing heaven to fill the room, making its atmosphere and resources available to those present. After the death of Billy Graham, amidst all the tributes and reflections on his life and ministry, the evangelist and activist Christine Caine tweeted:

> *I went to a Billy Graham mission in San Diego and literally bawled my eyes out for the entire hour that people streamed down the aisles to respond to the invitation. I had never seen or experienced anything like it in my life. The anointing was indescribable. I was marked forever.*[2]

Atmosphere changer

A time came when King Saul's spiritual state had badly deteriorated. God had stopped blessing him and had actually sent a tormenting spirit which used to seize him. He would then become not only extremely morose, but unpredictable and violent. Meanwhile, one of Saul's advisers knew of the young man David and his worship on the harp. He had presumably experienced first-hand the atmosphere of God's presence around him. He had the creative idea that as the harmful spirit began to affect Saul, David could be asked to play and worship, and

actually counteract the negative effects of the spirit. He understood that somehow the atmosphere of heaven came when
David worshipped – he imagined it could change the spiritual
dynamics in the heart of the troubled king. Saul, amazingly,
agreed to the experiment and David was duly brought in to
the court. It went as predicted, so David briefly became the
king's official worship leader. Saul loved him and for a while
was transformed by his influence.

I believe God was demonstrating something profound to Saul
through this arrangement. God had rebuked Saul for trying
to rule the kingdom of Israel by following his own human
instincts, rather than daily asking God for direction and following him. Saul's determination to do it his own way led him
far away from God's favour and blessing. David's arrival at
court was actually a gift from the God of grace: an opportunity
for Saul to humble himself and repent and get himself back
into relationship with God. The smart move would have been
to keep David close, develop a lifestyle of worship himself, and
finish his reign well.

Saul and David were both given the *same anointing* by Samuel
and by God. Both were dramatically changed when the Holy
Spirit came on them. Tragically, Saul slipped back into the
'I did it my way' human vanity trap, whilst David continued
to pursue intimacy with and reliance upon God. Saul may be
compared to the church leader who becomes self-sufficient,
confident in his or her natural gift – good planning, knowledge
of the Bible, counselling and diplomacy skills. They know that
they have departed from the intimate walk with God that they
once enjoyed. They feel dry and jaded. Then God exposes them
to a man or woman of the Spirit, who is like a David – maybe

a worship leader, who refreshes their heart, causing some of the old feelings to return. This process must then bring about a humbling change of heart or it will end in envy and the desire to destroy or remove the David.

Smelly worship

Jesus is at the house of a wealthy Pharisee. Surrounded by attentive men – the great and the good – a stream of life-impregnated words full of beauty and wisdom pour from his lips. The room is supercharged with expectation and wonder at the presence of Immanuel; God with us.

Suddenly, this intense spiritual atmosphere is shattered. A woman has barged her way into the room. She has been crying – her hair is down and her makeup is a mess as the tears stream down her cheeks. She gathers up her skirts as she clambers awkwardly over the legs of the men sitting on the floor listening to Jesus. This is embarrassing. She was clearly not invited to this select meeting – her behaviour lacks any scrap of decorum or respect for those gathered. As if she could not possibly make more of a scene, she pulls from her robe an ornate jar carved from alabaster, filled with pure nard, and smashes it on the floor. On her knees, at the feet of Jesus, she scoops up this richly-perfumed ointment from the floor with her fingers and spreads it all over Jesus' naked feet.

She is so far past caring what anyone present is thinking, her tears mingle in with the perfume as she anoints the Anointed One. Sobbing, she worships the Beloved, using her hair and hands to smear the ointment over the Christ, smeared by

God the Father. None of the guests have a clue about what is going on – they are outraged. They are offended by the 'sort of woman' (Luke 7:39) she is, but they are also offended by the extravagance. John records Judas voicing what others had been thinking – 'This is so wasteful! This ointment was valuable – it could have been sold for a year's wages and the money used for the poor. It's now useless – half of it on Jesus and half of it in the hair of some prostitute! Grrrr!' (John 12:5, my paraphrase).

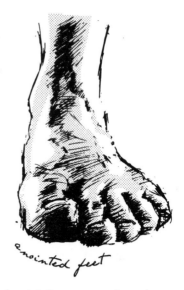

anointed feet

This woman did something the Pharisee who had invited Jesus had neglected to do. She anointed him. She was portraying in the language of prophetic worship the fact that Jesus is the Anointed One. Jesus rebukes his host for failing to show him an appropriate level of hospitality: 'I entered your house; you gave me no water for my feet, but she has wet my feet with her tears and wiped them with her hair. You gave me no kiss, but from the time I came in she has not ceased to kiss my feet. You did not anoint my head with oil, but she has anointed my feet with ointment' (Luke 7:44–46).

Honoured feet

At a meeting in the north of India, the friends of a young woman, newly married, asked me if I would pray for her.

She was wearing a veil – her face completely covered. These young women had come in from the houses nearby and joined the meeting hoping for a miracle or a blessing. As I moved to pray for the bride, she bent down reaching the floor – I assumed to pick something up. To my surprise, she touched my feet. Her friends all giggled at my surprise, telling me this was a sign of great honour given to elders, particularly by those newly married. I wept, moved by a culture of honour not known to us in the West.

The story of the woman anointing Jesus' feet is so alien to our Western culture. It didn't seem to fit with the culture of the day either. It was wasteful, emotional, messy, indecorous, undignified, inappropriate, and smelly! The others present in the room were shocked. We can imagine the videos and hashtags which would appear on social media if Jesus was a preacher today. Jesus himself was not only not bothered by the spectacle, he defended the woman and then said that she had done a beautiful thing to him.[3] I cannot help wondering how she knew that Jesus would like her to anoint his feet. I can't see any sneaky Old Testament prophecy saying that what God really likes is people anointing his feet . . . This woman brought her most treasured possession and wasted it on Jesus – he absolutely loved it. She poured out her broken heart to him – he received it as worship.

David understood what pleased the Lord – it wasn't a secret chord! Throughout the anthology of his psalms preserved in the Bible, we see again and again David pouring out his heart to the Lord. If he's doing well, he sings thanks to God, if his back is against the wall and he is surrounded by people wanting to slay him, he cries out to God, when he is confused, depressed, guilty – God hears something from his heart. Psalm 51 is a deeply moving outpouring from a heart broken by its own sin, yet it is not a litany of self-flagellation, neither is it hopeless despair. In fact, we see a revelation of what constitutes the true worship which moves God, which is then echoed in the actions of the woman with the alabaster jar:

> *Open my lips, Lord,*
>   *and my mouth will declare your praise.*
> *You do not delight in sacrifice, or I would bring it;*
>   *you do not take pleasure in burnt offerings.*
> *My sacrifice, O God, is a broken spirit;*
>   *a broken and contrite heart*
>   *you, God, will not despise.* (Psalm 51:15–17 NIV)

When our worship comes from deep within our hearts it touches the heart of God, who in turn releases the anointing of the Holy Spirit to us. Worship is a divine exchange where we delight in him and he delights in us, but we delight in him because he is already delighting in us! Jesus explained to the Samaritan woman he met at the well, that the Father is actually not bothered from where people worship him geographically, but he is very interested where the worship originates from in us. He said that the Father is actively looking for worshippers – it's interesting that he says worshippers, not worship *per se*, but worshippers who worship him from their spirit with integrity: spirit and life in agreement with the words coming from their lips.[4] His interest is in the heart condition of the worshipper, not so much the elegance or tunefulness of the worship. 'Behold, you delight in truth in the inward being' (Psalm 51:6).

Beauty rubs off

When the woman smeared the ointment all over Jesus' feet the fragrance of worship filled the room. It was a rare and beautiful fragrance. When Jesus left the house later that day he carried this smell with him wherever he went next. It would have lingered, possibly for days as it was an ointment which is absorbed into the skin. Not only did Jesus smell of the perfume, but so did the woman. The smell of the nard, the anointing of worship was in her hair, on her face and on her hands. A person passing by the woman, then later meeting Jesus, would instantly know that the two had been together. Her worship of the Beautiful One made her beautiful.

The anointing of worship is like the smell of the sacred incense used in the Tabernacle of Moses in the worship of God. It smells unlike anything else. This perfume clings to those who frequent the presence of Jesus. The oil with which he is anointed (which is, as we have said, the Holy Spirit) is smeared onto those of us who would come close to him. We then carry the fragrance of beautiful Jesus with us into our encounters with others – colleagues, family, strangers.

We assume the likeness of the one we gaze upon.

Esther was a foreign refugee with zero status who won a beauty contest. The prize was that she became queen (we could spend a long time thinking about the whole moral issues of such a contest, but that's for another day). The point was that she received intensive beauty treatments from a top beautician for a whole year before approaching the king: 'Six months with oil of myrrh and six months with spices and ointments for women' (Esther 2:12). She was soaking in the anointing to make her beautiful. The Holy Spirit is both our beautician and the oil mixed with spices, softening our skin and saturating us with his unique fragrance to make us beautiful for our prince, Jesus.[5]

The oil of joy

As a child, attending church (which was notably not joyful), on occasions my siblings and I would succumb to a fit of the giggles. The more we tried to suppress the laughter, the more likely it was that one of us would let out a snort which then triggered us all off into another helpless fit. This was more than my poor parents could bear and they would threaten to take us out of the service. The threat of the walk of shame hanging over us was usually just about enough to calm us down. Laughter, it seemed, was one thing which was clearly not acceptable to God! He seemed to like his house dark and sombre. In the light of Jesus, it's tricky to work out how church could have become so legendary at being dull.

> *You have loved righteousness and hated wickedness.*
> *Therefore God, your God, has anointed you*
>   *with the oil of gladness beyond your companions*
>   *your robes are all fragrant with myrrh and aloes and cassia.*
> (Psalm 45:7,8)

One of the ingredients of the anointing mixed in with the special perfume of Jesus is a lavish portion of joy. In fact, this psalm tells us that Jesus is more joyful than anyone else because God has anointed him. If we hang out with Jesus, we cannot help becoming joyful – the atmosphere of heaven rubs off onto us. Peter puts it: 'Though you have not seen him, you love him; and even though you do not see him now, you believe in him and are filled with an inexpressible and glorious joy' (1 Peter 1:8 NIV). Joy is listed as part of the evidence, or fruit, of having the Holy Spirit in our lives.[6]

A very cool thought

Here's a very cool thought: when God promised a son to the aged couple, Abraham and Sarah, God said his name would be Isaac, which means 'laughter'. Sarah laughed when she heard God speaking and making this promise to Abraham, but it was God's idea to call him Isaac. I love that God didn't call him Bible, or Prayer Meeting – God's promise, the ancestor of Jesus, the Anointed Messiah, was called Laughter! Church somehow, in the mists of time, became all respectable and formal and missed out on meeting the passionate, laughing, dancing heart of God.

Limited by language

The prophet Zephaniah describes God celebrating over his people when their fortunes are being restored.

> *The LORD your God is in your midst,*
>   *a mighty one who will save;*
> *he will rejoice over you with gladness;*
>   *he will quiet you by his love;*
> *he will exult over you with loud singing.* (Zephaniah 3:17)

The English language translations seem quite restrained when you look at the various meanings of the Hebrew words used. For example, *Strong's Concordance* gives the word translated here *exult* the following definitions: '*Gîyl, gheel*; or (by permutation) *gûwl*; a primitive root; properly, to spin round (under the influence of any violent emotion), i.e. usually rejoice, or (as cringing) fear: be glad, joy, be joyful, rejoice'.[7] It's quite a thing to imagine God being so excited about what is happening with his people that he might leap and spin around shouting and singing loudly.

When a political party wins a General Election, regardless of their nationality or which political persuasion they represent, grown-up men and women laugh and dance and sometimes weep. When a football team lifts the silverware, the crowd goes crazy: laughing, dancing, roaring and hugging each other. Grown men shed tears of joy! When a player scores a goal he puts his shirt over his head and runs up the pitch with his hands in the air, while his teammates jump on him. They are all laughing – laughter is a product of victory.

> *When the LORD restored the fortunes of Zion,*
> *we were like those who dream.*
> *Then our mouth was filled with laughter,*
> *and our tongue with shouts of joy;*
> *then they said among the nations,*
> *'The LORD has done great things for them.'*
> *The LORD has done great things for us;*
> *we are glad.* (Psalm 126:1–3)

> *Shouts of joy and victory*
> *resound in the tents of the righteous:*
> *'The LORD's right hand has done mighty things!'* (Psalm 118:15 NIV)

The church, in worship, is celebrating a much greater victory than winning the Champions League. What can I say? Maybe we should run around with our shirts over our heads!

(Yeah! I know, decently and in order.)

Jumping Jesus

Jesus was really excited when he sent out seventy-two disciples and they returned with stories of how God had been moving through them! Again, the Bible modestly says that Jesus 'rejoiced in the Holy Spirit' (Luke 10:21), but Dr Strong tells us that the word translated here *rejoiced* comes from two words, one meaning 'much' and the other meaning 'to jump, gush or spring up'.[8] Jesus was absolutely ecstatic when his students got it and started doing the stuff! Paul and Barnabas on their first apostolic trip together had been having a great time preaching in some of the cities in what is now Turkey. They had been really successful and many had been affected by the message and had received Jesus. When it dawned on their Gentile audience that the good news of Jesus was actually for them as well as the Jews, they became super-excited and full of joy![9] The preachers were making such an impact in the city of Antioch that their enemies stirred up some influential people who drove them out of the district. Luke, the reporter of the story, tells how they shook the dust from their feet – a symbolic act, shaking off responsibility for the lives of the people who had rejected them – and then headed off to the next stop on their tour, Iconium.

But here's the fun bit: Luke writes, 'And the disciples were filled with joy and with the Holy Spirit' (Acts 13:52). This is the evidence of the Christing – they were anointed with the same oil of joy as Jesus: a joy that was not based on how well things were going, or how popular they were. These guys were full of the oil of joy – they lived in the Christing. Their normal was to be filled with joy, not gloom. It is one of the biggest turn-offs when I see gloomy Christians, or find myself in gloomy meetings. Gloominess is not next to godliness. It's also worth pointing out, that God did not suddenly get a sense of humour in the New Testament. In fact God lives in his own climate, which is one of perfect, undiluted joy. We know that God laughs at his enemies:

You make known to me the path of life;
in your presence there is fullness of joy;
at your right hand are pleasures forevermore. (Psalm 16:11)

He who sits in the heavens laughs;
the Lord holds them in derision. (Psalm 2:4)

But the Lord laughs at the wicked,
for he sees that his day is coming. (Psalm 37:13)

Full of glory

For centuries certain brands of the church seem to have out-lawed emotion. Services have been stripped of any outward expression; distilled into precise forms of words and behaviour codes leaving no opportunity whatsoever for the biggest sin of all: emotionalism. The result is a kind of spirituality which feels remote, unconnected, sterile – religious. It is hardly surprising that people assume God is remote and unconnected. Modern science has done exactly the same. We have been told that our very existence was caused by natural events which spontaneously started happening purely by chance, billions of years ago – we are drifting on a tiny planet in an immeasurably vast, trackless universe and our lives have no meaning or significance whatsoever. God, on the other hand, tells us that he is uniquely interested in the earth; that he created the human race to be his representatives on this azure gem; ambassadors of heaven among the creatures he had made. He tells us that he created us like himself. He gave us the same range of emotions. When he created us he was so happy, he was rejoicing over us at the same time:

> *Then I was constantly at his side.*
> *I was filled with delight day after day,*
>   *rejoicing always in his presence,*
> *rejoicing in his whole world*
>   *and delighting in the human race.* (Proverbs 8:30,31 NIV)

God stood back and admired his work and saw that it was very good. He was totally thrilled with what he had made. Sin – the desire to do it our way rather than stick to God's design – was the poison that brought sadness and gloom into the world.

The anointing is all about the Christed ones returning the climate of heaven onto the earth. There is enough dreariness on the earth already, without the church adding to it and giving it a Christian name and address! Joy is not a luxury. Joy is a product of being filled with the Holy Spirit. Paul famously coins the phrase 'the fruit of the Spirit' in his letter to the Galatians. Joy is as inseparable from the fruit of the Holy Spirit as is love. The anointing of joy is actually part of God's glory. If we want to see God's glory on the earth, we must expect joy. Here's that statement from Peter again: 'Though you have not seen him, you love him. Though you do not now see him, you believe in him and *rejoice with joy that is inexpressible and filled with glory*' (1 Peter 1:8, emphasis added).

It was the anointing with the oil of joy that kept Paul and Silas worshipping God whilst they were in prison. It is the oil of joy that enables us to 'count it all joy' when we meet the various kinds of trials referred to by James. It is the oil of joy which transforms a dull job into a delight, or a long layover at an airport into an opportunity to share Jesus . . .

Joy that is inexpressible and filled with glory! This is not a theological concept; this is an emotion we feel! This is the human fully alive.

Let's pause and reflect . . .

I hope some cats have been released among some theological pigeons! Let's think about some of these ideas:

1. Have you ever been warned about the unreliability of feelings?
2. Have you ever fallen in love?
   • Did you conduct a risk/benefit analysis before entering a relationship with the person who had become the object of your affection?
   • Did you find yourself a little swept along by your emotions?
   • Did everyone agree with you, and did that matter?
3. Have you ever attended a football match as a fan?
   • Did you cheer when your team scored a goal? Did you risk a fist pump?
   • Were you experiencing intense emotion – maybe a tear in the eye?
4. What would your alabaster jar equivalent be? Think how you might give something costly to Jesus in worship. Would it be:
   • A song from your heart, sung out loud?
   • A physical item that you value?
   • A dance, hands lifted, kneeling, prostration – something way out of your comfort zone?
5. Whose love is more extravagant, the love of a mother expressed to her newborn, or God's love for you and me?

6. What moves us about the love of a mother?
   You might like to try this prayer:

Holy Spirit, please accept all of me as an instrument of worship. Use my mind, my creativity and my whole range of emotions to produce fresh ways of expressing my love for Jesus. Make me ever bolder as I approach him and less bothered about what others might think of me as I do. Let his perfume be all over me, let me smell of Jesus as I walk through town, show up for work or interact with my family.

12: More, Please?

Can I become more anointed?

Oliver Twist, the little orphan boy in Charles Dickens' novel, famously finished off his bowl of food and then asked for more. This is the big question for me: is my Holy Spirit anointing quota non-negotiably rationed by God, or do I get to ask for more? Does everyone who receives the Holy Spirit get the same dose and that's it?

There are some really cool things we can say, straight off the bat. Firstly, the Holy Spirit is God. He is therefore infinite. We will never ever exhaust his power or use up his potential! We know for sure that God's mercies are new every morning, his love is unfailing, his ways are higher than ours – everything about the Holy Spirit is big, great, magnificent and wonderful. Secondly, the apostle Paul tells us to eagerly desire spiritual gifts: 'Pursue love, and *earnestly desire* the spiritual gifts, especially that you may prophesy' (1 Corinthians 14:1, emphasis added). Paul does not encourage us to politely desire, or privately wish for.

I have heard people say that we should desire the Giver, not the gift – it is super-important to note that we cannot have the gifts of the Holy Spirit without the Holy Spirit himself. But, God responds to hunger: 'Blessed are those who hunger and thirst for righteousness, for they shall be satisfied' (Matthew 5:6). British politeness is a very strange thing: we apologise when someone bumps into us; we are also taught to say 'No, thank you' when offered a second helping. There is no room for this odd kind of false modesty around the Holy Spirit – pretending we are full when really we are empty. We should not be afraid to express our hunger for his presence, as did the poet who wrote: 'As a deer pants for flowing streams, so pants my soul for you, O God' (Psalm 42:1). He was so thirsty for God he imagined the thirst of a deer fleeing from the hunter panting desperately for water. Or Psalm 84:2, 'My soul yearns, even faints, for the courts of the LORD; my heart and my flesh cry out for the living God' (NIV).

Talented

Thirdly, God is not fair. He is entirely just, but that is quite different to our human idea of fairness. Jesus told the story of the boss who gave to each of his servants a different number of talents.[1] They did not each receive the same quantity – that does not sound fair. The returning boss, a metaphor for the returning Lord, was not interested in how many talents each received, but rather what they *did* with their allotted portion. We are often puzzled as to why God heals some people and not others. However, the God who made the universe without any helpful advice from me, also distributes the visible expressions of the Holy Spirit based on his own unique frame of reference: 'While God also bore witness by signs and wonders and various miracles and by gifts of the Holy Spirit distributed according to his will' (Hebrews 2:4). The same applies to the gifts of the Holy Spirit, 'All these are the work of one and the same Spirit, and he distributes them to each one, just as he determines' (1 Corinthians 12:11 NIV).

The parable of the talents has been a subject of preaching a million times. We have even adopted the monetary term *talent* as an English word to describe a person unusually good (I was going to say gifted) at a particular skill. It is used in relation to anything from mathematics to playing the violin. Surprisingly, a talent amounted to about twenty years' wages for a labourer – a lot of money. If we imagine twenty years' pay, in gold coins, in one payment, that's one talent. That seems to put an entirely different spin on the whole parable. Jesus has given us such a massive treasure in the anointing – the person of the Holy Spirit – even if we think we have less of a talent quota than someone else, we are still loaded! Our job now is to steward the anointing before Jesus returns and use what we have received to release the kingdom of heaven on the earth.

Never-ending supply

The first and second books of Kings are a sometimes exciting and sometimes painful read, but we find a great story in 2 Kings chapter 4. The stage is set as a tragedy: a widow, whose husband had been a prophet, is left in chronic debt following her husband's death. The creditor has demanded full repayment or has threatened to forcibly take the poor woman's two sons to make his slaves. She sets out to find the prophet Elisha and pours out her tale of woe. He asks her what she has left in the house – what asset does she have? Her answer seems pitiful, 'Your servant has nothing in the house except a jar of oil' (verse 2). Pitiful, unless we see the truth behind the story. She has oil. In her own eyes she is penniless and in debt to someone with no mercy. In the eyes of the prophet, however, she is in possession of a priceless commodity. Oil – the anointing – is the very thing which powers the kingdom of heaven on the earth. It is the very resource which makes the difference between the sons and daughters of the kingdom and the children of this world.

The prophet instructs her to send the boys round to all the neighbours to gather up as many empty pots, pans and receptacles as they can get their hands on. In her dingy humble home, there is no furniture, there are no ornaments, no pictures on the walls, just bowls, jars, buckets, cups, vases, cooking pans, jugs, and pitchers – oh, and one jar of oil. 'Shut the door,' she tells one of the boys, and the miracle begins. Slowly, tentatively, she pours the contents of her jar into the first bowl . . . miracles sound obvious afterwards, but I bet you could have heard her heart beating as she emptied that modest jar into a bigger bowl. As it became clear what was happening, and the oil was visibly multiplying, the boys started to up the pace – quickly gathering up the next container and passing the empties to be filled, then carefully placing the full vessels on a level surface to preserve every drop.

This is such a fab story! It's a great illustration of the infinite resources of God. It's an encouragement for us to expect miracles of multiplication, but it's also a picture of how God loves to pour out the Holy Spirit into empty vessels – empty people, that is. This is exactly what happened at Pentecost, at the house of Cornelius, Azusa Street, and has happened at every point in history where the Holy Spirit has swept through a community. The story teaches us to treasure times where the Holy Spirit is particularly moving, not to push through with *our* agenda, but to allow him to complete his. This story teaches us the true value of the anointing. The anointing releases our children from slavery and changes everything, giving them a hope and a future. The widow in this story is a prophetic picture of the church. Her very existence hangs on being faithful with the anointing of the priceless Holy Spirit.

Double portion

Let's stick with Elisha for a little longer. He was the servant and disciple of Elijah. Elijah was a legend in his own lifetime. He was the lone guy on the top of Mount Carmel who challenged the massed prophets of Baal to a showdown, calling fire down from heaven before the baleful glare of King Ahab. Ahab was the sell-out king who had caved in to the idolatrous ways of his evil wife, Jezebel, leading the whole nation miles away from God. Jezebel was so evil and manipulative, her very name makes pastors shudder to this day. Elijah along with Moses were the monumental figures, who of all the great characters in the Old Testament were the ones chosen to meet with Jesus on the mountain where Jesus was transfigured (more later). Moses died when he went up a mountain to meet with God one last time but no one ever found his body, whilst Elijah didn't even die – he was to be taken up to heaven in a chariot of fire. So cool, but a tough act to follow!

In the hours leading up to Elijah's exit from earth, Elisha is very aware that his master will be taken from him anytime soon, so sticks to him like glue. Elijah seems determined to shake him off and gives him numerous opportunities to leave, but the young man refuses to be diverted. After a final miracle – parting the water of the Jordan river with a single whack from his robe, enabling them both to walk across on dry ground – Elijah gives Elisha the offer of a lifetime: '"Ask what I shall do for you, before I am taken from you." And Elisha said, "Please let there be a double portion of your spirit on me"' (2 Kings 2:9). Elijah's response to the young padawan was not, 'Don't be silly, that's not how it works . . .' or any other such put down; rather, he replied, 'You have asked a hard thing; yet, if you see me as I am being taken from you, it shall be so for you, but if you do not see me, it shall not be so' (verse 10). In recent years there have probably been a million conferences offering a double portion of God's Spirit – it's easy to be sceptical. However, if a double portion is not really a thing, I wonder what was going on between these two prophetic giants.

The story is truly astonishing. The old prophet and his young assistant are walking and talking – presumably exchanging the kind of words close friends share when they know they will not see each other again. Suddenly, they are interrupted by a whirlwind of blazing horses whipped on by fiery angels riding chariots made entirely of flames. We read this stuff in the pages of the Bible and I'm sure we filter it out – this is not a normal Friday afternoon at the office . . . Elisha presumably staggers backwards to avoid being scorched and shields his eyes as he watches his beloved mentor swept up into the clouds in one of the chariots. As he stares intensely into the sky, trying to see another glimpse of the flame riders, he sees a flapping piece of fabric falling towards him. He recognises the cloak of his master. This is not just an essential fashion item for the aspiring prophet, this is the symbol of authority, which for years had rested on the shoulders of the older man. Elisha, returning home, approaches the Jordan river and shouts, 'Where is the LORD, the God of Elijah?' (2 Kings 2:14). He thwacks the waters and they part for him just as they had for Elijah earlier that day. He throws the mantle around his own shoulders and is instantly clothed in the spirit of Elijah. The other prophets see him approaching on his way home and say, '"The spirit of Elijah rests on Elisha." And they came to meet him and bowed to the ground before him' (2 Kings 2:15).

Just for a second, let's consider this story alongside the Acts 2 account of Pentecost:

1. Jesus had been taken up to heaven, leaving his boys wondering how on earth they were going to cope.
2. There was the sound of a whirlwind.
3. Fire appeared over each of the disciples.
4. The mantle (anointing) of Jesus fell on them.
5. They were filled with boldness and the Spirit of Jesus.

Without the mantle of Elijah, Elisha was just a bald guy with a beard and sandals – without the Holy Spirit, the church is just a weird kind of club with arcane rules.

It's not a competition, but the Bible records exactly twice the number of miracles for Elisha as for Elijah. It's not a competition, but God is not the rewarder of the mildly curious. Elisha demonstrated his hunger for the Spirit of God by not only faithfully serving the man of God in his lifetime, but also refusing to leave his side at the time of his impending departure. *A true hunger for the Spirit of God is actually hunger for the person of Jesus* – not a hunger for a sensational supernatural ministry, drop-dead accurate prophecies or 'high-level' miracles. In Matthew 7:22–23 Jesus rebukes those who wished to make a name for themselves performing miracles in his name, but who had not pursued intimacy with him. He actually brands them as workers of iniquity.

Trigger-happy

John tells us in his gospel account that Jesus was particularly fond of the two sisters, Mary and Martha, and their brother Lazarus. He was a frequent guest in their home, but also considered them close personal friends. The story recounted by John is very well known: Jesus hears from the sisters, 'Lord, the one you love is sick,' but then purposely delays two more days before going to their home to help. By the time Jesus does arrive Lazarus is beyond very sick, he's very dead and has been lying in the tomb for four days. Martha hears that Jesus is approaching, so gets up quickly and goes to meet him – she can't help blurting out, 'Lord, if you had been here, my brother would not have died.' Jesus reassures Martha that her brother will in fact live, but also reveals some profoundly important pieces of information to her which are now considered major planks of Christian theology: 'I am the resurrection and the life. Whoever believes in me, though he die, yet shall he live, and everyone who lives and believes in me shall never die' (John 11:25–26). Jesus asks if she believes this; her response is absolutely perfect: 'Yes, Lord; I believe that you are the Christ, the Son of God, who is coming into the world' (verse 27). There should be trumpets and choirs of angels at this point! Peter received a gold star and was upgraded to Rock level, when he correctly identified Jesus as the Christ. But Martha does receive her dead brother back to life.

Martha has seen, by revelation, that Jesus is not just a great guy to have stay in your home, but he truly is the Messiah, the Christ, the Anointed One – the Son of God made flesh, alive in our world.

Martha then fetches her sister, Mary, saying that Jesus is asking for her. Mary quickly jumps up and rushes out of the house to meet him. Falling at his feet, her words of greeting to Jesus are identical to those of her sister a few minutes earlier, 'Lord, if you had been here, my brother would not have died.' His response to Mary, however, is noticeably different from his response to Martha. 'When Jesus saw her weeping, and the Jews who had come with her also weeping, he was *deeply moved in his spirit and greatly troubled*' (John 11:33, emphasis added). In this chain of events we see four powerful emotional reactions in Jesus: firstly, he is deeply moved in his spirit and greatly troubled, then he weeps (verse 35). In verse 38, he is deeply moved again, then finally he cries out in a loud voice (verse 43). We should never underestimate what is going on in this story – this is God himself in human skin being moved by a deep friendship with people. Ordinary people. The same voice that commanded, 'Let there be light', is now booming out through human vocal cords and commanding a decomposing corpse to quit rotting and get back on its feet.

There are a lot of very unhappy people involved in the mourning party, but it is Mary who seems to trigger the movement of the Holy Spirit in Jesus. The phrase translated 'deeply moved' in the ESV is translated as 'groaned' in the King James

Version, but *Vine's Expository Dictionary of New Testament Words* explains the Greek word, *embrimaomai*: from *en*, 'in', intensive, and *brime*, 'strength', primarily signifies 'to snort with anger, as of horses'. Used of men it signifies 'to fret', 'to be painfully moved'; then, 'to express indignation against'.

snorting horse

This is not very churchy language – snorting like horses. I'm guessing this kind of behaviour would be considered inappropriate in St Paul's Cathedral. Whatever it was Jesus was feeling, he was feeling it pretty strongly. This deep feeling seems to have been sparked by running into Mary. We do know from earlier in the story that Mary had a special connection with Jesus – she was willing to leave the important duty of hospitality to her sister in preference to sitting at the feet of Jesus whilst he taught.

The Jesus reflex

I was enjoying a conversation about hearing the voice of God with a member of our team called Keira. We discussed how some people hear God speak in an audible voice, whilst others experience stunning visions. I was saying, a little wistfully, that I tend not to hear an audible voice and have had not so many stunning visions (two). I have had powerful encounters with the Holy Spirit which have literally knocked me off my feet and transformed my life – some of which get a mention in this book – but most of my sense of direction comes from a growing awareness of the will of God somewhere in my gizzard – I know, I don't have one – or an instant feeling of peace on the one hand or disquiet on the other. Even when I am 'brewing' a prophecy, I don't have a booming voice in my ears, but I have an unsolicited thought that seems like a God thought, which then grows into something fully formed as I speak it out. I may only have the wispiest sense of a one-liner to begin with, but it can emerge into a profound word once I start to roll with it.

She then came out with, 'But surely, is it not possible to have so given your heart over to Jesus that your responses are like a Jesus reflex?'

We have rightly taken to heart the word from Isaiah 55:9, 'For as the heavens are higher than the earth, so are my ways higher than your ways and my thoughts than your thoughts.' It's actually very good news that God is way beyond us – the book of Job is a wonderful illustration of that truth. However, this book is about the miracle that is the Christing. In Acts 5 we read the story of a couple of believers who were swept along with the culture of selling property and giving the proceeds to the apostles to fund the adventure which was unfolding in Jerusalem. This couple sold some land and brought the money to the apostles, but kept some back for themselves. This was not wrong – they didn't have to give any at all. The problem was that they had agreed to tell a lie to make themselves look more generous than they really were. They reported to Peter that the sum they gave was the total price they received for the land. The story is quite shocking, as Peter asks first the husband and, later that day, the wife, if this really was the price they had received. Peter's Jesus reflex knew that their story was not the truth. His statement was that they had conspired to lie to the Holy Spirit. They had lied to Peter, but Peter was full of the Holy Spirit, the Christing, so they were actually lying to the Holy Spirit. It must have been a tough day for the young church as they buried Ananias and Sapphira.

On a more cheerful day, it was three in the afternoon and Peter and John were heading off to pray when they approached the guy who was always lying begging outside the gate of the Temple called the Beautiful Gate. It seems quite likely that Peter and John had seen him before – it's easy to get used to someone who is a regular fixture, with the same old issues, who keeps wanting something from us – but then the Jesus reflex kicks in. 'Look at us,' says Peter – I bet John was thinking, 'Uh-oh, I wonder what Rocky's up to now!' In that second, everything changes – the man looks up expecting money, instead this crazy guy is taking him up by his arm and commanding him to start walking. What's even more crazy is that he can feel his ankles and legs becoming strong as the Christing in Peter activates muscles and ligaments that atrophied in the womb!

I'm excited!

Lightning rods

There appear to be triggers which release the supernatural flow of the anointing, taking us out of the realm of our own natural abilities to operate in the realm of God's unlimited power and creativity. Certain people are like lightning conductors in the realm of the anointing. They are particularly tuned to the Holy Spirit and respond quickly when God begins to move. Mary seems to have been one such person for Jesus. These are the kind of people I love to hang around with – I know they will help me flip into the flow of the Holy Spirit's anointing, which is when the fun starts! They help me to be a better version of me; they stop me being ordinary, by co-conspiring to find that spring of life bubbling up in my belly.[2]

Compassion

Jesus had heard about the death of his cousin, John the Baptist, so took a boat ride to somewhere desolate where he could be by himself for a while. However, the news of his whereabouts leaked out and crowds came after him on foot. By the time he reached the shore there was a great crowd waiting for him. Matthew tells how when he saw the great crowd, 'He had compassion on them and healed their sick' (Matthew 14:14). He then went on to feed 5,000 plus people by multiplying a small packed lunch of five loaves and two fishes. In another place Matthew writes: 'When he saw the crowds, he had compassion for them because they were harassed and helpless, like sheep without a shepherd' (Matthew 9:36). It may be worth noting that Jesus did not invite everyone to a Picnic in the Park event; rather, he fed their spiritual hunger and healed their sick, so they were desperate to be near him. Later, Matthew records a similar miracle where Jesus feeds 4,000 men plus women and children. Again, it is compassion which triggered the flow of the anointing and the miracle. 'Then Jesus called his disciples to him and said, "I have compassion on the crowd because they have been with me now three days and have nothing to eat"' (Matthew 15:32). Compassion was the trigger which moved Jesus to raise the dead son of the widow at Nain at his funeral.

Compassion is deeply embedded in the heart of God – it is part of his nature. When our human hearts are touched by his divine compassion we feel his heart for people. Learning to move in the anointing is very much about responding to and getting into the flow of what God is doing already. This was exactly how Jesus operated. When the Jews questioned what he was doing he replied, 'Truly, truly, I say to you, the Son can do nothing of his own accord, but only what he sees the Father doing . . . For the Father loves the Son and shows him all that he himself is doing' (John 5:19,20). What God is doing is not a secret. He loves to reveal it to people who orientate their lives to listen and respond. 'The Lord GOD does nothing without revealing his secret to his servants the prophets' (Amos 3:7). Psalm 25:14 in the King James Version tantalisingly tells us, 'The secret of the LORD is with them that fear him.'

Anger

Surely anger could not be a legitimate trigger for the anointing? Paul and Silas have arrived in Philippi. They have gone in response to a dream, where Paul had seen a man calling him to come over to Macedonia to help. Things are going pretty well, they have met a businesswoman called Lydia who loved their message, received Jesus and opened her home for the apostles to stay and use as a base. The two guys are heading to the place of prayer by the river, when they are confronted by a demonised slave girl who starts shouting and saying, 'These men are servants of the Most High God!' Paul is not looking for demonic recognition as the basis of his ministry so tries to ignore it at first, but this happens day after day, until Paul is 'greatly annoyed'. He turns and addresses the demonic spirit, commanding it to come out of the girl. Instantly she is free. Her owners, who used the spirit of divination in the girl as a means of income, are furious and drag Paul and Silas in front of the magistrates who respond to the charges brought by throwing the preachers in prison (see Acts 16:16–19). Paul's irritation with the demonic attention-seeking had triggered him to act and move in the anointing. Remember Isaiah 61: 'He has anointed me . . . to proclaim liberty to the captives, and the opening of the prison to those who are bound.'

In 2017, in a city in Central Asia, I was ministering for ten days in a Catholic church where most people only spoke Russian or the local language. A thin young man who spoke very good English attached himself to me and immediately launched into a long monologue about how there was a conspiracy against him and it involved governments and so on, and on, and on some more. He was nervous and twitchy and did not look well. The next couple of days, he repeated the whole thing each time he saw me until I began to feel irritated inside – I felt his paranoia was a manifestation of some kind of oppressing spirit. In the end, I said, 'Let me pray for you.' I took him in my arms, holding him close whilst praying in tongues for a few minutes – hoping the Holy Spirit would do whatever was needed. The next day he came up to chat as before, but looked chilled and at peace. We enjoyed normal conversation and he never returned to the obsessive conspiracy talk again for the rest of the time I was in the city. He wrote to me (you have to read it with a Russian accent): 'After your prayer something good happened with me. I stop cursing people and spat in the streets. It is also good news.' This is really good news: freedom to the captives, triggered by – irritation.

One more: Peter. He was in Samaria, with John, laying hands on people so that they would receive the Holy Spirit. There was a local celebrity watching this phenomenon, as people were touched powerfully by the Spirit when the two apostles put their hands on them. This guy was called Simon. He was a magician, who had gained the title of 'The Great Power' due to his influence in the city. He liked what he saw and thought how it would add to his reputation if he could do the same thing, so asked Peter if he could buy the gift. Peter's reply seems to have a hint of irritation in it: 'May your silver perish with you, because you thought you could obtain the gift of God with money . . . Repent therefore . . . For I see that you are in the gall of bitterness and in the bond of iniquity.' The response of Simon was to humbly ask for prayer for forgiveness (Acts 8:9–24). Once again, Simon had been bound, in his case by bitterness and iniquity, then the anointing, triggered by a sense irritation in Peter, releases freedom to the captive.

Dare I say that God is irritated to the point of taking action when he sees demonic oppression keeping people bound and dysfunctional? We should not be surprised when the passionate God disrupts our respectable church and uses some Holy Spirit firepower to set the captives free.

Faith

A woman has been suffering from a severe gynaecological condition, causing her to be constantly bleeding for twelve years. She has spent a fortune paying for doctors to give her remedies which have universally failed, until now, finally, she has nothing. Then she hears about Jesus. Her condition makes her feel weak through anaemia, but she's also treated as an outcast as she is constantly ceremonially unclean, according to the law. She has faith, however, that if she can just touch Jesus, she can be healed without having to be seen by everyone and can be spared further embarrassment. Well, she presses through the crowds surrounding Jesus and bends down to touch his robes. Instantly she's healed. That moment, the bleeding stops, the miracle she has longed for for twelve years has happened. However, she is not ready for what happens next. Jesus stops dead in his tracks and says, 'Who touched my garments?' Oh boy, surely he didn't notice – but he's determined and is looking round to see who it was. She is well and truly busted! She comes trembling forward, falls on her knees and tells him the whole truth. The beautiful Jesus says, 'Daughter, your faith has made you well' (Mark 5:34). Here's the really cool bit: Jesus knew that the anointing had been activated, even though he had not intentionally released healing. 'And Jesus, perceiving in himself that power (virtue, KJV) had gone out from him . . .' (Mark 5:24–34). This woman's faith had triggered the anointing (remember, the anointing is a person, not a thing) without Jesus' conscious permission. Jesus had not prayed for her, laid hands on her or rebuked anything – he had not intentionally engaged with her at all. The point is that the Holy Spirit is the one who performs the miraculous act. He can be acting whether the ministering person is conscious of it or not.

We read that Peter's shadow fell on people and they were healed – maybe he was off to the market to buy some vegetables, and people were healed spontaneously as he walked by. We also read that Paul's tent-making aprons and sweaty handkerchiefs healed people when they were brought into contact with sick people. Let's never forget, the Holy Spirit is a person with a mind and thoughts of his own. Whilst he does love to work in partnership with human people – after all, that is what the anointing is all about, the Holy Spirit on human flesh – yet he is sovereign and completely able to move in ways that catch us by surprise. I could be preaching about worship, for example, with my mind fully engaged on that subject; meanwhile the Holy Spirit is healing someone's body in the congregation and I know nothing about it.

A person reaching out to God in faith evokes a response from the Spirit of God. A miracle is a transaction carried out by the Holy Spirit in response to the faith of a person or group of people. This miracle may or may not include a human intermediary operating as a minister. Watch what happens with Paul: Acts 14:8–11; Paul is preaching at Lystra. There is a man in the crowd who has never walked because his feet have been deformed since birth. He is not just in the crowd, but he is listening to Paul. The anointing in Paul (the Holy Spirit) has a flash of recognition that this guy has faith to be made well. Paul doesn't invite him forward for prayer; he calls out in a loud voice, 'Stand upright on your feet.' The guy doesn't get up slowly, he leaps up like a coiled spring – boom! This is the *dunamis* power triggered by the faith of the crippled man and the obedience to the anointing of Paul.

Whilst faith is most definitely a trigger, it is also true that cynicism is hostile to the anointing. Jesus, on one occasion, returned to his hometown of Nazareth and proceeded to teach in the local synagogue. The reaction of the local people when they heard his stunning wisdom and saw the miraculous signs was initially one of astonishment. This was followed by the kind of reasoning which is designed to bring the anointed person back down to our level: '"Is not this the carpenter's son? Is not his mother called Mary? And are not his brothers James and Joseph and Simon and Judas? . . . Where then did this man get all these things?" And they took offence at him' (Matthew 13:55–57). Matthew goes on to say that Jesus did not do many mighty works there because of their unbelief. Even Jesus, the most anointed person ever to walk the earth, was severely limited by human unbelief. This attitude is sneakily prevalent in the church in the UK at the present. We find it difficult to believe that anyone we know might be operating more powerfully than we are – we are sometimes even secretly pleased when we can debunk their stories of miracles.

Unbelief is a fire blanket which shuts down the supernatural power of the anointing. Cynicism is the pirate who hijacks our treasure ship on its way home.

Let's pause and reflect . . .

1. Think about your understanding of the parable of the talents. How does it change if you think in terms of the Holy Spirit as the talent you have received?
2. Have you sub-consciously put a ceiling on what you are now capable of as a Christed one?
3. Do you have co-conspirators who trigger you into the 'flow of the Holy Spirit'?
   - Does any of this make sense to you at all?
   - Do you prioritise time with this kind of person?
   - Do you spend the majority of your time with the 'fire-blanket' type?
   - What kind of person do you think you are, fire-starter or extinguisher?
4. Can you identify the Jesus reflex operating in your own life?

A prayer:

Dearest Holy Spirit, I repent of burying my talent in the ground. I am so sorry! Let me fully exploit all of the potential you have invested in me by taking up residence in my life. You are amazing, unlimited and so beautiful. Let me never again smother your fire by my apathy or unbelief!

Over and out (for now).

13: Flesh v. Spirit

Romans 8

I have read this chapter of the Bible hundreds of times, but find I keep coming back for more. The amazing thing about God's Word is that it is actually alive; God can speak to us through the same passage again and again – as many times as we read it. It is truly the gift that keeps giving! The letter to the Romans is widely considered the apostle Paul's masterpiece – whole books have been written on it, thousands of sermons have been preached on it. In this great chapter he describes the interaction between the Spirit and the flesh – that is, the natural human side of our human nature. He opens by saying that for those who are in Christ Jesus (that is, of course, in Jesus, the oily Messiah) there is no sense of condemnation hanging over us. There is no fear of impending doom, or rejection by God due to our sin, because Jesus has taken care of that. Paul describes how the equation of sin = death, is now cancelled by the law of Jesus (Spirit of life) = freedom. He says that being in Christ Jesus exempts us from the equation of sin and death.

Then Paul begins to explain and expound. In verse three: 'For God has done what the law, weakened by the flesh, could not do. By sending his own Son in the likeness of sinful flesh and for sin, he condemned sin in the flesh.'

Let's try to unpack that.

The Law – that is, the written down requirements for God's people to live by, as spelled out in the Old Testament – was from God, therefore we know it is good. In fact, David says, 'The law of the LORD is perfect' (Psalm 19:7). This perfect law, however, was limited in that it was given to dodgy human beings like me. Although the law defined God's perfect standard, it failed to make anyone perfect.[1] No-one has ever succeeded in living up to the standards set by the law (except Jesus). We may not have committed murder, but who has never secretly coveted their neighbour's stuff – her husband, his BMW, or their holiday? In the Ten Commandments, this is commandment number ten (Deuteronomy 5:21): the joker in the pack. The other nine commandments deal with my actions, but this one judges my hidden thoughts. A court of law would find it difficult to convict me of the crime of coveting, but God observes my most secret inner mind space. Paul says that the law was weakened by the flesh. My humanity teamed up with my unerring tendency towards sin means that a list of commandments is pretty soon going to become a list of indictments showing exactly where I have failed.

Counsel for the prosecution

Jesus once asked an expert in the law to summarise his understanding of the Commandments. His reply was, 'You shall love the Lord your God with all your heart and with all your soul and with all your strength and with all your mind, and your neighbour as yourself' (Luke 10:27). Jesus applauded his summary, but actually he had put his finger on the very problem. By his definition each of us has epically failed. Not one of us have consistently loved God like that, or loved our fellow human in the way we love ourselves. Enter Satan, whose name means Accuser. He is pretty hot on the law – in fact, he is the sinister legal prosecutor obsessed by a mission to condemn the whole human race to eternal separation from God our Father. He wants to keep us all outside of God's presence, today and tomorrow and forever. On the one hand, if we feel condemned today we will never embark on any ambitious exploits for God, on the other hand if we are condemned forever – what a tragic loss to the loving Father.

It's easy to make a superficial judgement and say that the law of God was a failed experiment, but that is to entirely misunderstand its purpose. Firstly, the law was essential to pull together the twelve tribes of Israel to make them into a governable nation. It gave them a distinctive value system that set them apart from all the other tribes, ethnic groups and nations living at that time in history. But it also has a much higher purpose in that it demonstrates just how much we humans need Jesus – it shows us that we can never achieve God's standard even by doing our very best. As the King James Version of the Bible puts it, 'Wherefore the law was our schoolmaster to bring us unto Christ' (Galatians 3:24 KJV). Jesus taught how sin is not just crossing a boundary – transgression or trespassing – rather, sin comes from my heart. I will have crossed the line in my heart long before I put the impulse into action.

The law can influence my behaviour, but it cannot change my heart.

The Sin Club

So then, the flesh of humanity – our human nature, with its instincts and drives – weakened the law, preventing it from making us right with God. Human flesh was first sucked into sin through the actions of our common ancestor, Adam. Since then, every human to be born has been a fully signed-up member of the Sin Club. Theologians like to call this our fallen nature. In spite of all of this, as we have said, the anointing is for flesh and blood. It is for us – people. Jesus did not send the Holy Spirit to fill angels, but human beings made of flesh. So on to verses three and four:

> *For what the law was powerless to do because it was weakened by the flesh, God did by sending his own Son in the likeness of sinful flesh to be a sin offering. And so he condemned sin in the flesh, in order that the righteous requirement of the law might be fully met in us, who do not live according to the flesh but according to the Spirit.* (Romans 8:3,4 NIV)

What the law could not make happen God did another way, by sending his Son, Jesus. Jesus came to earth as one of us – flesh and blood. He lived the life of a genuine flesh-and-blood human, but never signed up to the Sin Club. Because God was his Father, not Adam, Jesus avoided the family membership deal.

In our village, just up the road from the house we were raised in, there was an old abandoned cottage. We good Christian kids had talked ourselves into believing it was haunted. One day we scraped together all the bravado we could muster and decided to venture inside. It was super-creepy. Our hearts pounding, we began to climb the stairs – that is, until my sister grabbed the banister rail and it disintegrated in her hand. Terrified, we shot back out of the front door like scalded cats, never to return! When

scalded cat

such a building falls derelict, it will be declared unfit to live in – it is now condemned. This particular house was duly demolished to make way for a new development. Jesus had a fully human body, but demonstrated that a human who is filled with the Holy Spirit does not have to sin. He condemned sin – he declared it unfit for us to live in anymore.

Having brilliantly succeeded at the human life, scoring 100 per cent, Jesus returned to his Father, from whence he sent the Holy Spirit to bring revolution to our lives. In fact, when we receive Jesus, God considers us *in Christ* – that is, in the Perfect Human, who is the Anointed One. He anoints us – fills us with the Holy Spirit – and our membership of the Sin Club is revoked. It becomes as though we are now fully compliant with the law. Not only is that so, but now we have a choice – we are no longer bent towards sin. Interestingly, one of the Hebrew words translated iniquity means bent, or trained like a vine, to sinfulness.[2] We now get to choose to live according to the (Holy) Spirit. Verse four of our chapter says that we now actually begin to fulfil the requirements of the law as we live out this new version of our lives, according to the Spirit. The supernatural power of Jesus is now living in us to enable us to live the kind of life which pleases God.

Alternative version

If my friend Dave witnessed a horrific car crash and then shared his experience with me, I might then recount the story to someone else saying, 'According to Dave . . .' I am describing his version of events. Someone else witnessing the same accident may have a very different version of what happened. If I choose to live according to the flesh, my life will follow the typical, unremarkable pattern of a Sin Club member. We could call this Version #1. If I choose, however, to live according to the Spirit, I will opt in to an entirely different version of my

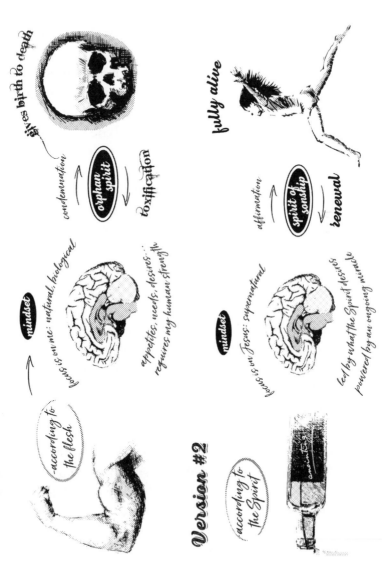

Version #1

according to the flesh

mindset
focus is on me: natural, biological
appetites, needs, desires...
requires my human strength

orphan spirit
condemnation
toxification

gives birth to death

Version #2

according to the Spirit

mindset
focus is on Jesus: supernatural
led by what the Spirit desires
powered by an ongoing miracle

spirit of sonship
affirmation
renewal

fully alive

life, like entering a parallel universe. We could call this Version #2. Because the Holy Spirit I am listening to and living according to is the Spirit of Jesus, my life will begin to look more like his. I will be listening to and agreeing with what the loving Father has to say about me, not the constant grinding condemnation coming from the father of lies. I have not stopped being a flesh-and-blood human being, but I am living in the anointing of the Holy Spirit. This is the greatest adventure!

Paul goes on to spell it out – I can continue to live according to the flesh, Version #1, but it will end up producing death. It always does. It's an all too common experience for pastors – we watch people who started well sliding into spiritual death as they choose to go back to living according to the flesh version.

Mindset: set mind

Paul describes a partnership between the mind and the Spirit. In verses 5 and 6 he explains how the person living according to Version #1 will have their mind set on the flesh, whilst the person living according to Version #2 has their mind set on the Spirit. The result of Version #1 is death, whilst the result of Version #2 is life and peace. We have been given the Holy Spirit to perform a transformational miracle in our hearts, as prophesied by Jeremiah (Jeremiah 31:33), where the law of God, with his preferences, is coded into our hearts; but the mind is required to cooperate with this miracle. In recent years a lot of research has been carried out on the brain. It is exciting to learn that the brain remains 'plastic', that is, able to change shape and develop, throughout the large part of our lives. Dr Caroline Leaf has written describing how our brains are far more healthy and effective if we fill them with God thoughts. She explains how thoughts become established pathways in the brain, actually changing the physical shape of our brains. She also describes the effect of negative thinking, how toxins such as cortisol are released into the brain by anxiety, fear or judgement, bringing death to our precious dendrites – the gossamer branches of our brain cells which make up the thinking part of us.[3]

Just as a bodybuilder sculpts his or her body into the image they admire, so we intentionally or unintentionally sculpt our brains into the image of that which we admire. Later in Romans, Paul urges his readers to not be pressurised into the thinking of the corrupt world, 'But be transformed by the renewing of your mind' (Romans 12:2). Here is the apostle Paul, writing 2,000 years ago, chiming in with 21st-century neuroscience, whilst tying up with prophecies, some of which were already 700 years old when he was alive, from the greats like Isaiah, Jeremiah and Ezekiel.[4]

Freedom

We have seen how the anointing in Isaiah 61 is all about freedom – freedom for captives and release to those who are bound. Paul writes to the Corinthian church:

Now the Lord is the Spirit, and where the Spirit of the Lord is, there is freedom. And we all, with unveiled face, beholding the glory of the Lord, are being transformed into the same image from one degree of glory to another. For this comes from the Lord who is the Spirit. (2 Corinthians 3:17,18)

We said earlier that the anointing, or the Christing, is not a thing, it is a person – the person of the Holy Spirit. In this passage from Paul's second letter to the Christians at Corinth, Paul helps us get hold of an important piece of theology: 'Now the Lord is the Spirit'. The Lord, Jesus, the Christed Messiah – he is the Spirit. Let's now just back up and put Paul's comments into context. Moses stood in the presence of God for days and days at a time and when he returned to the camp his face shone with God's glory. In fact, his face was so bright that the people's eyes hurt when they looked at him. Today, we would issue people with welding masks or protective goggles before visiting the man of God. Back then, the solution Moses came up with was to wear a veil to cover his face. However, it does seem that Moses was more concerned about the people seeing the glory fade, than the frying of retinas. Paul makes the comparison with us gazing on the glory of God as Moses did as we encounter him through the Holy Spirit in worship and in our personal times spent with him. As we gaze on him we are transformed to the point where we begin to reflect his glory. Listen to this extraordinary account of a Russian monk, St Seraphim of Sarov:

> *The description of Motovilov of the transfiguration of Seraphim is something unique in Russian mystical literature: 'I said: "I cannot look at you, Father, because lightnings stream from your eyes; your face has become more brilliant than the sun and my eyes cannot bear it."'*[5]

The freedom of the Holy Spirit is freedom for me to gaze on the loveliness of Jesus – to be transformed by repeated encounters with his glory. In Christ, we are invited to stand on the Rock and experience God up close, just like Moses and Elijah. The difference for us is that we have been invited to come boldly, as sons and daughters, knowing his perfect love which casts out fear.[6]

Back to the flesh

Whenever we start talking about sins of the flesh in church, it seems to be in relation to sexual sin. Although, the term could equally well be used for over-eating, laziness and a number of other fleshly pitfalls. Historically, the church has had a tricky time dealing with this area of life and in helping people deal with the issues arising from the fact that we are indeed sexual beings. In recent years, the many sexual scandals relating to church personnel have left the church with even less confidence to speak about sexual issues. The design of our bodies means that we are physically equipped to engage in sexual activity from the time puberty hits us onwards. Sex was God's idea in the first place – a great idea – designed to bring joy and bond couples together providing stable families for children. It is a perfect gift from God which has been serially hijacked by our enemy. Christians can often be guilty of either implying that sexual sin is the worst possible sin, or at the other extreme, turning a blind eye to it to avoid being judgemental, because we see being judgemental as the worst sin ever.

Paul does a great job with this subject in his first letter to the Corinthians. He has just brought a tough word about a guy in the church who is sleeping with his father's wife (chapter 5).

In chapter 6, he goes on to make the point that our body has desires, but these desires can enslave us into areas such as drunkenness, gluttony and sexual immorality. He then makes the most profound point: 'The body is not meant for sexual immorality, but for the Lord, and the Lord for the body. And God raised the Lord and will also raise us up by his power. Do you not know that your bodies are *members of Christ?*' (1 Corinthians 6:13–15, emphasis added). Actually, I didn't know that for a long time! He is saying that our blood-and-guts bodies which enjoy food and pleasure and sex are actually physical components (members) belonging to the Anointed One – the most holy Christ.

I know, it is not a little mind boggling, but then it gets even more intense. In verse 16, Paul describes how sexual intercourse makes two people joined, as *one flesh*. He then goes on to say, 'But he who is joined to the Lord becomes *one spirit with him*' (verse 17, emphasis added). Anyone thinking that being a Christian is just another lifestyle choice might wish to reconsider at this point – that's clearly not how God views it! God thinks he has the right to inhabit my body and treat it as his temple (verse 19). The reason sexual sin is destructive is because it attempts to unite the dwelling place that God has chosen with a third party, or, in the context of Paul's argument, a prostitute. 'Shall I then take the members (body parts) of Christ and make them members of a prostitute? Never!' (verse 15, parenthesis added). This seems shocking, particularly if we have relegated the Christian life to some kind of vague spirituality. God, however, seems very happy to use graphic sexual imagery to make his point.

The point is that the anointing – the person of the Holy Spirit, who is God himself (yes, I am stressing the point) – joins himself to the person who has surrendered to Jesus. He begins the miracle of transformation at that point; changing us into the likeness of Jesus. He expects us to keep the temple of our bodies exclusively as his dwelling place (this is holiness), but equally, he helps us by making us desire what he desires, creating a lifestyle which pleases him.

Legalism

In spite of all that we have said, legalism is often the solution applied to sexual sin. It is the idea that if I try extra hard to keep the law in all its details I will succeed in being pleasing to God. We can be trying to be super-holy by applying legalistic methods, and using judgemental language against others, whilst losing the battle ourselves with sexual issues. The best way to live free from sin of all kinds is to occupy ourselves with pursuing Jesus and daily surrendering to the direction of the Holy Spirit – renewing our minds with wholesome stuff. We soon get to realise that being close to Jesus and full of the Holy Spirit is so preferable to the jaded desire and self-reproach that comes with sexual indulgence.

Bewitched

Paul's letter to the Galatian church declares all-out war on the whole issue of legalism. He insists that trying to please God by sticking to the requirements of the Jewish law is like getting sucked into witchcraft: 'O foolish Galatians! Who has bewitched you?' (Galatians 3:1). These non-Jewish believers were being pressurised to having their men circumcised like their Jewish brothers. They were trying to adopt the Old Testament laws as a way of being more acceptable to God. For God this is no better than pagan superstition. This was, indeed, going back to a Version #1 existence. Paul sees how this trend is going to wreck the whole Gentile church if he does not make a course correction urgently. 'For all who rely on the works of the law are under a curse, as it is written: "Cursed is everyone who does not continue to do everything written in the Book of the Law"' (Galatians 3:10 NIV).

Paul takes this thought into areas which seem almost opposite to our instincts, and popular Christian belief. He fiercely states that we cannot persuade God to do miracles by our trying to be extra good – by being super-law-abiding Christians – we cannot make ourselves any more likely to be filled with the Holy Spirit by trying harder. He then pulls Abraham into the ring. Father Abe didn't have the Bible – neither the Old nor New Testament – he didn't even have the law in a written down form. Even so, God counted him as righteous: acceptable and pleasing to God, because he believed what God had promised. The whole point of the gospel is that we can't save ourselves however much we try to keep the law – we need a Saviour. This carries on being true, even once we have prayed the 'sinner's prayer', been baptised and started speaking in tongues – we still can't make it alone. We needed God's gift, his grace, to save us; we also need grace to live. We cannot become pleasing to God using the efforts of our flesh. We please God when we make use of the gift he has given us – the Holy Spirit.

A quick word on Grace

Grace has become another well-worn word of the Christianese language. It is the English translation of the Greek word *charis*, which simply means *gift*. It is the whole essence of the Christian gospel. It is not complicated, or magic. It simply, but amazingly, means that people who deserve nothing good from God – only punishment for sin – get treated like sons and daughters of God, firstly in this life, and then in the life to come. And it's all because of Jesus!

The Holy Spirit is a gift – always has been, always will be. We could say that he is the personification of grace – if grace were a person it would be the Holy Spirit. We will never deserve the sweet anointing of his presence; the gentle stirring in the heart which makes us want to worship. The initial baptism in the Holy Spirit is a gift to a new believer who, seconds before, stepped out of a life of self-pleasing and sin and stepped into Christ. The ongoing, day-by-day anointing and filling is as much a gift as the original down-payment. Just think of the lunacy behind the thought that I might somehow make myself *more* deserving of the Spirit of the Eternal God, Creator, Genius, Mastermind of the Universe living in my shabby Christian life!

We stay filled the way we became filled in the first place: by humbly coming to God – putting our hands out to receive. We do this day after day, hour after hour, believing that he is a good, good Father, who loves to give good gifts to his children.

The life of the Spirit is powered by grace.

Let's pause and reflect . . .

1. Read Romans 8 and 1 Corinthians 6:12–20.
2. Have you tried to live the Christian life as a list of rules? How did it go?
3. Reflect on the thought that God considers your body as his temple.
   - How might that affect your attitude to taking exercise, rest and diet?
   - How might it affect how you refer to your body? For example, do you ever say things like 'I hate my legs/bottom/belly'?
   - How might it affect your view of sex?
   - How might it affect your choice of TV viewing?
4. If the temple built by Solomon was so beautiful, and so much care went into building it, how might God consider the temple of your body?

The Running Prayer (I often pray like this when I'm running)

Lord, I give you my hands: (wave your hands, optional)
Let them be your hands today.
Let them be healing hands,
Touch and heal people through my hands today.

Lord, I give you my feet: (kick your feet, optional)
Let them be your feet today.
Let me walk in your footsteps;
Let me go where you are going.

Lord, I give you my eyes:
Let me look with compassion today,
Let me look with purity,
Let me see what you see in people today.

Lord, I give you my lips,
Let me speak your words today . . .

Lord, I give you my ears . . .

Lord, I give you my imagination . . .

(and so on).

14: The Cloud

pillar of cloud by day

Baptised into Moses

Moses, as we have said before, was a pretty special guy. He enjoyed the most astonishing level of relationship with God – a relationship not experienced by any of the other prophets (Numbers 12:8). He saw God up close, not from a distance – it's true to say that the people of Israel did not fully appreciate just who it was they had at the helm. Under Moses' leadership a whole nation possibly numbering around one and a half million people were not only rescued from the tyranny of institutionalised racism and the wretchedness of slavery in Egypt, but adopted their own legal system, and survived a forty-year-long camping expedition in the desert.

The people were led by the presence of God in the visible form of a cloud in the daytime and a huge pillar of fire at night.

You can imagine the excitement the first time the people saw the cloud and then watched as it changed to blazing fire at nightfall – it must have been truly spectacular! The experience of Israel's Red Sea crossing is taken by the apostle Paul as a metaphor for baptism. 'For I want you to know, brothers, that our fathers were all under the cloud, and all passed through the sea, and all were baptised into Moses in the cloud and in the sea' (1 Corinthians 10:1,2). They came out of the oppression in Egypt, passed through the sea, and lived under the cloud. This is a picture of the gospel of Jesus: supernatural rescue from the brutal dehumanising slavery of sin, baptism into Jesus and baptism in the Holy Spirit (the cloud). You will notice that redemption from slavery was an event, as was the baptism in the sea, but the baptism in the cloud was the continuous state in which the people continued to dwell.

Likewise, baptism in the Holy Spirit is not a one-off event that happens once and we're done – speaking in tongues, and all sorted – rather, this is a place where we dwell. We were designed to live under the cloud of God's presence. For the entire time the nation of Israel lived under the cloud, although geographically they lived in a desert, they experienced heaven on earth. This is open heaven – remember the law of first mention in chapter two. God protected them from their enemies and wild animals. Their shoes never wore out, neither did their clothes become threadbare. Fashion stood still for forty years! I guess they continued wearing the fine clothes they were given by their neighbours when they left Egypt – the best dressed nomads in the Sinai Peninsula. No-one fell sick, no-one grew weak in that time either. What did happen, though, was that a generation of unbelievers, who had refused to take God at his word, died off, one by one. Meanwhile, growing up under the discipleship of Joshua and Caleb, was a new generation with a different spirit.

round up the chicks

Following the cloud

The cloud and the fire were not only the visible evidence of God with them as a nation, they were also a means of navigation. God issued very strict instructions that when the cloud of his presence came to rest the people were to set up camp. Whenever the cloud moved on – whatever time, day or night, they were to dismantle everything, gather up the sheep, goats and chickens, hunt for the children, or wake them up, and be ready to follow the cloud. They may have been camping in a good spot for weeks, everything set up just as the pro-camper likes, then the cloud moved. Someone noticed and started shouting, 'The cloud's moving – look, it's moving!' Throughout the whole community, each tribe, clan and family suddenly became obsessed with getting packed up and moving as quickly as possible in order to keep up with the Presence of God as it shifted to another location. The lives of nomadic herds-people have always centred around finding good pasture for their animals, a supply of clean water and some safety from the unwelcome attention of raiding parties or bandits. Instead, for the nomadic Israelites in the desert, their primary focus for forty years was watching for the cloud and then following where it went.

However, here is something so profound. The cloud was moved by the supreme sovereign will of God. Everything else about the Israelites' lives was secondary. But take a look at this:

> *Now Moses used to take the tent and pitch it outside the camp, far off from the camp, and he called it the tent of meeting. And everyone who sought the LORD would go out to the tent of meeting, which was outside the camp. Whenever Moses went out to the tent, all the people would rise up, and each would stand at his tent door, and watch Moses until he had gone into the tent. When Moses entered the tent, the pillar of cloud would descend and stand at the entrance of the tent, and the LORD would speak with Moses. And when all the people saw the pillar of cloud standing at the entrance of the tent, all the people would rise up and worship, each at his tent door. Thus the LORD used to speak to Moses face to face, as a man speaks to his friend. When Moses turned again into the camp, his assistant Joshua the son of Nun, a young man, would not depart from the tent.* (Exodus 33:7–11)

The nation of Israel worshipped in response to Moses' relationship with God. 'Whenever Moses went out to the tent, all the people would rise up, and each would stand at his tent door.' The man of God approached the tent of meeting and everyone knew that during this time God would be extra close. '*When Moses entered the tent, the pillar of cloud would descend* and stand at the entrance of the tent, and the LORD would speak to Moses' (verse 9, emphasis added). The cloud of God's presence, which a whole nation followed for forty years, moved in response to Moses. Moses was a friend of God – but God was so eager to spend time with Moses, that he responded to Moses making the first move. 'Thus the LORD used to speak to Moses face to face, as a man speaks to his friend' (verse 11). There was an open heaven for the fledgling nation of Israel because of Moses' friendship with God. An open heaven is a product of the anointing on the life of a friend of God.

God's order

On one occasion, Moses had to deal with a rebellion where some bona-fide priests, Korah, Dathan and Abiram, rebelled against Moses' and Aaron's leadership. Korah argued that the whole nation was holy, not just Moses and Aaron – a good point, but Korah twisted the truth to make a case for rejecting Moses as their senior leader. It resulted in a showdown where God emphatically chose Moses and Aaron (Numbers 16). The three men along with their wives and children were swallowed up alive as the earth split open and they fell in. The other 250 men who had joined forces with these rebels were killed by the fire which leapt from the condemned men's priestly censers and burned them up. That was a tough day in the camp. The community had just watched as the rebels were divinely punished, but how do you get over the sounds of the screams of the wives and little ones as they disappeared into the earth, or the smell of 250 guys burning? This sparked further hostility and grumbling towards the two brothers God had anointed to lead. Once again, the cloud moved in response to Moses: 'And when the congregation had assembled against Moses and against Aaron, they turned toward the tent of meeting. And behold, the cloud covered it, and the glory of the LORD appeared' (Numbers 16:42). This time God had come in judgement.

God, the awesome Unapproachable One had turned up to defend his friend. A plague broke out which was only stopped when Moses ran though the camp with a censer with fire from the altar, frantically interceding for the people – again! God stopped the plague in response to Moses' prayers, but 14,700 besides the original rebels died that day.

There are two points here: firstly, the presence of God and an open heaven are an immense privilege. The most extraordinary things are possible in that environment of God's glory, but this is God we are dealing with. It is possible to get familiar with his presence and glory and begin to disregard it. But God is holy. And he's God! The second point is that God is faithful to his friends. Don't let's mess with God's order and let us not mess with God's friends.

Dig this

Part of the kit for the Israelite camping under the cloud was a spade. They were required to take it with them when they needed to use the bathroom. They headed off into the nearby scrubland to do their business, then used the spade to dig a hole and bury the evidence. The reason was that God was in the habit of coming from time to time and walking through the camp – he would check over his people like a shepherd does, and keep them safe.

Because the LORD your God walks in the midst of your camp, to deliver you and to give up your enemies before you, therefore your camp must be holy, so that he may not see anything indecent among you and turn away from you. (Deuteronomy 23:14)

It is awesome to think that God himself actually walked through the camp. This is like it was in the very beginning with Adam and Eve – God used to meet with them and walk with them, discussing the gardening business and sharing his heart for them. That really is the most amazing thing about this verse, but we are amused and distracted by the instructions of how to deal with large quantities of community poop. The point is, God cares about how we live. He wants his people to be holy; that is, special and different, as we have said previously – set apart for him. Of course he sees our natural activities – after all, he designed each function of our bodies – but he does want us to live better than animals. God is not embarrassed by human excrement, but when we live together it is pleasing to him that we deal with it in a way that makes communal living bearable and healthy. I am sure he wholeheartedly approves of sewers.

Today, God is still very interested in how we live together. In fact, the anointing and favour of God can be totally compromised by our communal lifestyle. Peter tells husbands that we should love our wives and treat them considerately, or with honour. 'Husbands, in the same way be considerate as you live with your wives, and treat them with respect as the weaker partner and as heirs with you of the gracious gift of life, *so that nothing will hinder your prayers*' (1 Peter 3:7 NIV, emphasis added). Let's get away from the obvious argument about who may be actually stronger, to the main point: if married men are inconsiderate and exploit any physical advantage, or even social advantage we may feel we have, to abuse or disadvantage our wives, God will choose to become deaf to our prayers. This principle must surely extend to men, married or otherwise, in relation to women in the working environment, or wider society. God also becomes selectively deaf when we turn a deaf ear to the cries of the poor, denying our social responsibility:

'Whoever closes his ear to the cry of the poor will himself call out and not be answered' (Proverbs 21:13).

Open heaven culture

There are clearly certain environments which God prefers to visit to others. In order for us to enjoy an open heaven like Moses did, our first priority has to be to make him our first priority. There are endless legitimate things we can do with our time – many things which in themselves are not wrong or evil – but pursuing Jesus must become number one. In Paul's letter to the Ephesians, he spells out some of the choices we should make. For example:

> *And do not get drunk with wine, for that is debauchery, but be filled with the Spirit, addressing one another in psalms and hymns and spiritual songs, singing and making melody to the Lord with your heart, giving thanks always and for everything to God the Father in the name of our Lord Jesus Christ, submitting to one another out of reverence for Christ.* (Ephesians 5:18–21)

Getting drunk with wine is just a poor and lazy substitute for being filled with the Spirit. It's what people resort to when they can't get the real thing. When we are enjoying being filled with the Holy Spirit we feel euphoric and in love with everyone, but there's no hangover! We choose it because it's so good. We choose to sing spiritual songs which dwell on just how amazing Jesus is, not because he has forgotten, or is insecure, but because as we gaze on him, we become like him (see chapter 11). As we pursue his presence, we begin to naturally choose the things he likes. My second daughter has begun to attend the occasional football match. She has never been remotely interested in football, or standing outside in the rain, but her fiancé plays football. In fact, he's from Latin America where football is a religion, so I suspect she will have to watch plenty more. We make the choice not to get drunk with wine because it conflicts with the Holy Spirit. Meanwhile, giving thanks always and for everything is a continual reminder that God the Father is the source of every good thing which comes into our lives.

Gratitude is linked with humility. It is an attitude of giving honour. I am sad when I see people who see themselves as important, particularly Christians, disregard the little people who serve them. When we attend a conference, the way we treat the stewards, or the parking attendants, shouts a loud message about our hearts, as does the way we interact with the staff who serve us when we eat out. Along with gratitude is the attitude of submission to one another out of reverence for Christ. That is, of course, reverence for the Anointed One.

We want the anointing in our lives – we will need to learn how to submit.

Unity

Let's take a look at another super-famous piece of scripture:

Behold, how good and pleasant it is
when brothers dwell in unity!
It is like the precious oil on the head,
running down on the beard,
on the beard of Aaron,
running down on the collar of his robes!

It is like the dew of Hermon,
* which falls on the mountains of Zion!*
For there the LORD has commanded the blessing,
* life forevermore.* (Psalm 133)

In this passage, dwelling together carries a sense of sitting down and settling – making our home there. It is the Hebrew word *yashab*. It is also in Psalm 91:1: 'He who dwells in the shelter of the Most High.' This is not the occasional moment of unity where we successfully pulled off a joint initiative with another congregation, or when we have a monthly service with a number of other churches in the area. These are good things and may help us move towards where we need to be, but the unity described here comes when we have made our home together. *Yashab* has a sense of marriage, of habitually lurking around the same place – of waiting together. I'm going to suggest that unless we have learned to submit *to one another* our marriage is going to be pretty grim. Likewise, living together in true unity requires that heart of submission.

But look at the prize! The anointing, the sweet aromatic oil of the precious Holy Spirit is glugged all over us. On the head, the beard, the robes – this is not just a little bit of anointing, this is a whole gallon of extra virgin dripping from us! Not only that, but the Lord has commanded the blessing – life forevermore. The blessing is guaranteed by the Lord. His life flowing among us forever. That's the corporate anointing, the unstoppable life of God flowing among a group of people, with the fragrance of the anointing dripping from them everywhere they go.

So worth it!

It is so interesting to ponder these familiar verses. The High Priest is Jesus. The anointing is the Holy Spirit – he is all over Jesus. The oil runs down his beard onto his robes. The church is the body of Christ; the body of the Anointed One. Notice, the oil of the anointing flows to the lowest place – the place of humility and brokenness.

Marriage anointing

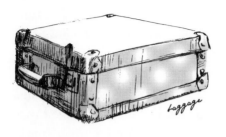

Marriage was God's idea. According to the apostle Paul, marriage is an earthly representation of the romance and ultimate union between Christ (I hardly need to repeat it: the Anointed One) and the church. Today, marriages inside and outside of the church seem to be suffering an all-time low, with more than half of the marriages in the UK ending in divorce. Marriage definitely does have certain built-in challenges: firstly, the person I will marry will be fundamentally genetically, biologically and psychologically different from me; secondly, I am flawed from the outset! I bring baggage, my spouse brings baggage – most marriages start out looking like a left-luggage depot. But, if God delights to pour his Spirit on brothers who dwell together in unity, surely he delights in unity between a husband and wife.

Malachi, the final book of the Old Testament, has some powerful points to make on the subject. The prophet rebukes the people for playing fast and loose with the covenant of marriage.

It would seem that some were bringing domestic violence into the home and expecting that God would not notice. As we have already said, God is keenly interested in how we live our private and home lives. He watches the whole soap opera – never misses an episode, so he is fully aware of the way we treat our spouse and our children. Malachi asks, 'Did he not make them one, *with a portion of the Spirit in their union*? And what was the one God seeking? Godly offspring' (Malachi 2:15, emphasis added). Let me attempt a paraphrase:

> *Didn't God design marriage to make two people into one whole person? He even gave each married couple a special measure of his Holy Spirit anointing to make their uniting supernaturally better. And what is this God of perfect unity looking for from the whole marriage thing? He wants children to be born into the world who know who they are and know that they are loved by their parents and by God, the good, good Father.*

God designed marriage in the same way he designed the universe – he designed it well and he designed it to work. On the sixth day of creation, God surveyed all that he had made and saw that it was very good – he had just made the man and the woman.[1] The culmination of Project: Creation was a man and woman, purpose-built for each other. A matching pair. Malachi wrote his prophecy before the Holy Spirit was poured out at Pentecost. He wrote before Jesus came and made the New Birth possible. He described a relationship, enshrined in a covenant, where two fundamentally different individuals, a man and a woman – the same kind, but hard-wired to be different – would find a oneness in their physical and emotional unity which was a reflection of the oneness within God himself. He would use broken people to display through their marriages a picture of the tender romance between the anointed Christ and the church. He designed this unique relationship to be the cradle which nurtured new sons and daughters in the sacrificial love required to make a marriage work, but he gave a measure of his supernatural Spirit to help us succeed.

In the house Anna and I shared when we were first married, there were two steps down from a small passage into a kitchen. One particular evening we had been having a strong disagreement about something, but on this occasion I knew that I was right – Anna was simply not seeing it! I walked from the living room and stepped down into the kitchen, and as I did, the Holy Spirit spoke to me. It was so clear – almost audible: 'She's right, you know.' I couldn't believe it! 'Whose side are you on?' I asked, but I knew that I was not going to get a reply. There was no point arguing – I turned straight around and went back into the room where Anna was still smouldering. 'The Holy Spirit has just told me, you are right,' I said. She was lost for words. 'I'm sorry, I was wrong,' I continued. All the tension disappeared and we slipped back into unity again. To this day, I have no memory of what the big issue was, but I do vividly remember the portion of his Spirit in our marriage that day.

So many times he has helped us in our marriage: resolving our differences (too many to number), rescuing us financially, helping us when we have completely run out of ideas with our children, healing our bodies, guiding our decisions – we owe him everything. I am a great believer in marriage. However, I don't believe we get a perfect marriage just because we're Christians, but I do believe the Holy Spirit is poured on us when we stand in front of God and say those vows. I do believe that he helps us make it a success if we are humble enough to submit to his anointing.

Let's pause and reflect . . .

1. Think about a nation living directly under the cloud of God's presence. What might that mean for your nation? Write a list and begin to intercede for your nation/city/ community accordingly.
2. How is the communal living going?
   - at work?
   - at university/school?
   - at home?
   - at church?
3. What is the church unity looking like in your town? Is it a token combined service once a month, or are relationships between congregations deepening to look more like Psalm 133?
4. How do we achieve unity without losing our identity?
5. Do your city leaders pray together frequently?
6. How is the unity in your marriage?
   - How do you submit to one another and still have leadership?
   - What happens if you disagree over something really important?
   - When did you last say, 'I'm sorry, I was wrong'?

15: Breaking Yokes

Troubles

Northern Ireland is part of the United Kingdom; it is also part of the island of Ireland. The state of Ireland is a separate entity. Ireland broke free from British rule in 1922 and was known as the Irish Free State. It became a republic in 1949. Living in the North were large numbers of mainly Protestant people who remained loyal to Britain. They were the majority. There was also a large number of predominantly Catholic people who wished for a united Ireland ruled from Dublin. Sadly, irreconcilable tensions between the two communities had existed for centuries. The British Government had used brutal methods to maintain the rule of law, human rights had been abused, and the Irish people have long memories. They traced this sometimes bloody, often heavy-handed oppression to the days of Oliver Cromwell and his invasion in 1649. In the 1960s these underlying tensions erupted into a period of bloody violence in Northern Ireland with murders, bombings and atrocities carried out by paramilitary groups claiming to represent both sides. British soldiers patrolled the streets with machine guns, the politicians raged, the media gobbled it up, whilst the people of Northern Ireland put their heads down and tried to have some kind of life.

There were certain triggers which activated the reaping of whirlwinds. One such trigger happened every year on the same day in July, the Orange March at Drumcree. This was one of a series of marches carried out by the members of the Orange Order, a society which prided itself in its loyalty to the British Crown. Marches are still held all over the province in the summer months, but this particular march had become infamous. The contentious issue was that the route the march would take involved walking along the predominantly Catholic Garvaghy Road. This was seen by the resident groups who had strong republican sympathies as insulting and provocative. The trigger was activated on a number of occasions resulting in severe rioting. In July 1996 a Catholic taxi driver was shot dead at Drumcree.

The same year, at a major Christian youth festival in England, whilst trying to sell books, I happened to meet a man called Morris who lived in Portadown, the town adjoining the tiny village of Drumcree. He was trying to bring Jesus to a certain group of young people from his community who spent their evenings on the banks of the River Bann drinking Buckfast Wine. He had been a secondary school science teacher and knew many of the boys and girls by name. I optimistically suggested that I could help and he invited me to bring a team of young people over to join him for a few days. This was the beginning of something far bigger than we could have ever imagined. After our first visit I returned later with a friend to spend a few days fasting and praying for a sense of what God was doing and what he wanted us to do. We asked Morris to take us to the field where all the action kicked off in the summer. As we walked around the field praying we sensed that God wanted us to come back for some serious intercession.

Two weeks before the date of the march we returned with a team of around twenty worshippers and pray-ers to fast and

pray for a week. The team
was an unusually eclec-
tic mix of God's fabulous
family. We slept in tents in
the field whilst hosting vis-
itors and conducting our
worship and praying in a

marquee. It rained the whole week. The longer we went without food, the colder it felt, even when wearing every item of
clothing we had brought with us. People joined us in the big
tent to pray from both the Catholic and Protestant communities and from north and south of the border, some came from
Scotland! The presence of God was awesome – we saw people
receive Jesus and others physically healed. We watched a woman's bent lower leg straighten out in front of our eyes. The sight
of two English teenage girls from our team lying face down in
knee-high wet grass, weeping and crying out for people they
would probably never meet, was something I will never forget.
Another thing I will never forget was taking the bread and wine
with Catholic and Protestant believers as we broke our fast on
the last day. The peace I felt was so intense, it felt as if I had
died and gone to heaven.

Good Friday

That year, the Drumcree march was peaceful and therefore
not particularly newsworthy, in spite of the presence of news
reporters from around the world. The following Easter weekend, on Good Friday 1998, the historic Good Friday agreement was signed. It was a massive breakthrough and marked a
political turning point. We knew that God had drafted us in to

play a small part in something he was doing on the big stage. That summer, however, things turned ugly again at Drumcree, so in 1999 we returned, this time with our own marquee as no-one would allow us to hire one! Once again, twenty or so of us fasted and prayed for a week; this time we scheduled to break our fast the Saturday before the Sunday march. Small groups went out into different parts of the town, walked up and down the streets, we met with local politicians and clergy, where they were willing to see us.

On the Thursday morning at about 5.00 a.m. I was awakened by one of our team telling me that the Army were ploughing the bottom section of the field we were camped in and that the officer in charge wanted to talk to me. I dragged myself out of the sleeping bag, at which point my leg suddenly cramped and I promptly fell over in front of the officer – I like to make a good first impression! Now there was not a single chance of looking as if I had it together. He seemed to be asking us to leave, but I said that we still had work to do. We called my dear friend Clive back at home and asked him to pray – I didn't want to be reckless and put the lives of our team in danger unnecessarily, and this officer was clearly expecting trouble. He told us we were free to stay as we were on private land with permission from the farmer. He would do his best to rescue us if everything went nuclear, but would not be able to save our precious marquee if someone did decide to torch it.

Back in Dorset, Clive prayed with the husband of one of our team and they confirmed our feeling that we should stay.

I should cut to the chase. We continued on. For the Saturday morning we had invited people to attend a meeting we called a

'Solemn Assembly'. We didn't really know what we were doing except following the leading of the Holy Spirit. So much of what I have learned about intercession came by actually being in the firing line. On the Friday evening we sent most of the team to a safe house some miles away and a small number slept in the marquee to look after it and all our stuff. We took the sides down from the big tent so that we were clearly visible to anyone who might be suspicious that we were concealing an arsenal. We survived the night. In the wee hours, some guys circled the marquee slowly in a high-powered sports car, but thankfully left us alone. The Solemn Assembly saw people from all over the Province, people from the Republic and even from Scotland gather to repent to each other for the gravity of the situation our respective dogmas had allowed to exist. It was deeply moving to watch Catholic leaders in reconciliation share alongside Protestant ministers. We repented, forgave, hugged, wept and prayed. Again, we broke the fast with Holy Communion. When we were done the people spilled out onto the field and chatted as they strolled down to the barbed wire and barricade. Such a contrast – the fear and suspicion displayed in camouflage and weapons, compared to such heavenly unity demonstrated by the atmosphere of peace and calm among the people who had been praying. Psalm 133 was definitely in operation that day.

We took down our tents and left. The next morning, the day of the much-feared march, the BBC reporter stood in the field and said, 'I am here in the field at Drumcree . . . the atmosphere is one of peace'. Oh yeah!

Jesus, you are awesome!

Always interceding

If we portray the devil as a chief prosecutor, attempting to bring accusations against God's dearly loved children, the good news is that there is most definitely a pro advocate speaking in our defence. The writer to the Hebrews tells us that Jesus himself always lives to make intercession for those who come to God through him.[1] Interceding for someone, is taking up their case and talking to the judge on their behalf. It is acting as a go-between, or an intermediary in a dispute between two parties. This is an anointed priestly role; this is what Jesus does right now. He is the great High Priest standing in heaven refuting the claims made by Satan, the accuser, against God's people. It's so good that we have Jesus!

Robert Henderson makes the point that spiritual warfare is often more of a courtroom battle than hand-to-hand combat with the enemy. Thankfully, the warfare we were engaged in at Drumcree did not involve bullets or Molotov cocktails, although it easily could have. We can see a powerful picture of exactly this kind of courtroom battle actually taking place in the book of Zechariah.

> *Then he showed me Joshua the high priest standing before the angel of the LORD, and Satan standing at his right hand to accuse him. And the LORD said to Satan, 'The LORD rebuke you, O Satan! The LORD who has chosen Jerusalem rebuke you! Is not this a brand plucked from the fire?' Now Joshua was standing before the angel, clothed with filthy garments. And the angel said to those who were standing before him, 'Remove the filthy garments from him.' And to him he said, 'Behold, I have taken your iniquity away from you, and I will clothe you with pure vestments.' And I said, 'Let them put a clean turban on his head.'*

So they put a clean turban on his head and clothed him with garments.
And the angel of the LORD was standing by. (Zechariah 3:1–5)

In this vision Zechariah is given insight into what is going on behind the scenes in the life of a really significant spiritual leader of the time – Joshua, the son of Jehozadak was the first High Priest to be appointed after the Jews returned to Jerusalem from captivity in Babylon. He had really important work to do, and God had invited him to have access to the courts of heaven (see verse 7). Satan, however, is seen accusing him to God. We do not know from the story how much Joshua is aware of this, but we can safely assume that he feels somewhat daunted by the task before him, in that the angel of the Lord needs to solemnly assure him. It is usual when God calls us to perform a task for him, for us to feel unworthy. In this vision Joshua is dressed in filthy clothes. He has just come up from captivity in the pagan land of Babylon, he has been steeped in the culture and conditioned by its values – he needs a radical heavenly makeover.

Zechariah, who is having the vision, is now being drawn into the process of intercession. He sees the angel giving Joshua new clothes and he pipes up, 'Give him a clean turban!' (my paraphrase). So they put a clean turban on his head. The removal of his dirty clothes is a representation of his culture of sin being taken away – the new turban is a picture of his whole thinking and mindset being transformed. This vision shows, firstly, Satan bringing the accusation; secondly, the Lord himself rebuking Satan and declaring his intentions for Joshua; thirdly, angelic intervention; fourthly, a human intercessor being brought in to contribute to the process.

Priestly intercession

We talked about the priestly anointing in chapter 4, but we talked mainly about the priestly role of blessing. The other role is that of mediation. In Paul's first letter to Timothy we read, 'For there is one God, and there is one mediator between God and men, the man Christ Jesus' (1 Timothy 2:5). The writer to the Hebrews explains that Jesus is now the High Priest who opened up the way for us to go boldly, direct to God:

> *Therefore, brothers, since we have confidence to enter the holy places by the blood of Jesus, by the new and living way that he opened for us through the curtain, that is, through his flesh, and since we have a great priest over the house of God, let us draw near with a true heart in full assurance of faith, with our hearts sprinkled clean from an evil conscience and our bodies washed with pure water.* (Hebrews 10:19–22)

Therefore we could say that the priestly role of mediator has been thoroughly done by Jesus. Yes, but the scripture is clear that he still wants his friends involved in the process of bringing his purpose about on the earth. He still wants us to preach the good news, he still wants us to heal people, prophesy, bless and pray.[2]

At the most extreme moment in Jesus' life on earth, he was in prayer. In the garden of Gethsemane, hours before his betrayal and crucifixion, he was in the deepest anguish looking forward to the moment when he would endure the full measure of God's hatred of sin. 'And being in anguish, he prayed more earnestly, and his sweat was like drops of blood falling to the ground' (Luke 22:44 NIV). At this time Jesus particularly wanted his special friends to pray and back him up. He left the other disciples and took Peter, James and John, the three to whom he seemed to be closest, a bit further. Mark tells us how he began to be 'greatly distressed and troubled. And he said to them, "My soul is very sorrowful, even to death. Remain here and watch"' (Mark 14:33,34). Sadly, the guys couldn't stay awake, in spite of their best intentions. Jesus had no choice but to go through his darkest hour alone. However, even in this time of great sorrow he demonstrated his awesome ministry of intercession. John chapter 17 records what is considered the most significant priestly prayer of Jesus – he prays for his disciples, and looks forward to future generations, praying even for those as yet unborn.

Groaning

Back to the Drumcree scenario – we did not have a clue how to pray appropriately. We did know that we had received the anointing of the Holy Spirit, however, and were pretty sure he would know what to do. We made it our main business to worship Jesus and dwell in his presence. In that environment we could actually sense the atmosphere of heaven invading the earth. In heaven countless angels busy themselves carrying out the Father's will – I'm certain they helped us at that time, especially in the light of things I have found out since. A friend I now know, was working for the Government security forces at the time. She told us how they were acting on intelligence of a seriously high level of risk to the soldiers and police at Drumcree whilst we were there. Behind the scenes the situation was considered to be a powder keg. Without heaven's intervention, the story could easily have ended very differently.

We did a lot of groaning, a lot of praying in tongues – what else can you do when the situation is grave and you've run out of smart stuff to say? I'm so glad of Romans 8:26,27:

> *Likewise the Spirit helps us in our weakness. For we do not know what to pray for as we ought, but the Spirit himself intercedes for us with groanings too deep for words. And he who searches hearts knows what is the mind of the Spirit, because the Spirit intercedes for the saints according to the will of God.*

There is an oft-quoted verse which I'm going to add, even though it is a marginal translation, simply because it fits! 'And it shall come to pass in that day, that his burden shall be taken away from off thy shoulder, and his yoke from off thy neck, and the yoke shall be destroyed because of the anointing' (Isaiah 10:27 KJV).[3] Other translations go for the word *fatness* – that is, the yoke is broken because you have grown fat. We will consider the link with fatness and the anointing in the next chapter.

The Holy Spirit knows what is needed in each situation. When he recruits us for intercession, we do not need to have any prior inside knowledge at all, although he may choose to share knowledge with us. Here is a cool example. In 1994, South Africa was experiencing a major shift from Apartheid, the evil political system which gave power and privilege to the white minority and kept the black majority living in poverty and political powerlessness. The nation held its first general election where a Government of National Unity representing many different ethnic groups took the leadership for the first time. These were challenging times with tensions boiling up between the different ethnic leaders. A key figure refused to take part in the elections and threatened to jeopardise the fragile peace – Chief Mangosuthu Buthelezi, the leader of the Inkatha Freedom Party. He was a Zulu chief with great influence among the largest of the South African tribes.

It was a Sunday morning and we were in our church service when the Holy Spirit prompted us to pray that Chief Buthelezi would come to the table and bring his people into the nation-building process. We prayed furiously for maybe twenty minutes. The urgency lifted and we carried on with the service. We heard later that day that the chief's flight had been delayed as he was trying to leave the negotiations, refusing to participate any longer. During that period of time the plane was grounded, a Kenyan negotiator caught up with him and persuaded him to stay. He rejoined the negotiations and brought the Zulu nation on board. He was voted into the brand-new Government of National Unity as Minister of Home Affairs.

We found out later through a Kenyan friend that the negotiator was a Christian. We also learned that at the football stadium where the historic negotiations were taking place there was a room full of Christian intercessors praying and interceding through the whole process. We may never know why the Holy Spirit got us involved in that way, but it felt pretty good to think that we had been drafted in to influence the birth of a nation that day.

The Cyrus Factor

In his amazing prophetic book, Isaiah introduces a man who will not appear on the world stage until over 100 years later than the time of writing (Isaiah 44, 45). Many pages have been written by scholars and critics arguing how this section of the book must surely have been written after Cyrus, by someone other than Isaiah. However, I am going to assume that it was written by the prophet Isaiah and is, in fact, a prophecy. The Bible is full of prophecy. If we start chopping out bits that seem improbable because they are too accurate, we soon don't have a Bible. The whole section on Cyrus is absolutely fascinating and holds true to the themes we have seen which accompany other references to the anointing. In chapter 44:28, Isaiah reports God speaking of Cyrus: 'He is my shepherd, and he shall fulfil all my purpose', the purpose being to rebuild the ruins of the city of Jerusalem and the Temple. In chapter 45:1 we read: 'Thus says the LORD to his *anointed*, to Cyrus, whose right hand I have grasped' (emphasis added). Cyrus, the not-yet-born Persian king, is somehow the Lord's anointed, Christed (*mashiyach*) messiah. This man was to grow up in a pagan, non-Jewish environment and become king of a mighty empire, yet God would call him and anoint him for a greater purpose – to facilitate the return of a wave of Jewish exiles from Babylon to restore the heart of the Jewish nation from the previous desolation caused by Nebuchadnezzar's army. His role appears to be to break up the deadlock which has been keeping God's people in captivity:

> *I will go before you*
> *and level the exalted places,*
> *I will break in pieces the doors of bronze*
> *and cut through the bars of iron,*
> *I will give you the treasures of darkness*
> *and the hoards in secret places . . .* (Isaiah 45:2,3)

We have previously considered Isaiah 61, the passage Jesus claimed for himself, and seen how the anointing was to set the captives free. This is also true of Cyrus. What God goes on to say in the following verses is very cool:

> *For the sake of my servant Jacob,*
>   *and Israel my chosen,*
> *I call you by your name,*
>   *I name you, though you do not know me.*
> *I am the* LORD, *and there is no other,*
>   *besides me there is no God;*
> ***I equip you, though you do not know me.*** (Isaiah 45:4–5, emphasis added)

It seems that to begin with, Cyrus did not know God, but that through God's dealings with him he would come to know him: 'That you may know that it is I, the LORD, the God of Israel, who call you by your name' (verse 3). The prophet then goes on to describe how people all over the earth would realise that God had done this amazing thing. This is followed by a passage which illustrates the open heaven phenomenon, where heaven and earth seem to have a harmonious communication and flow, resulting in great blessing and fruitfulness on the earth.

> *Shower, O heavens, from above,*
>   *and let the clouds rain down righteousness;*
> *let the earth open, that salvation and righteousness may bear fruit;*
>   *let the earth cause them both to sprout;*
>   *I the* LORD *have created it.* (Isaiah 45:8)

We will take a look at this whole fruitfulness deal in a bit more detail in the next chapter. Isaiah even speaks of Cyrus having an evangelistic role, as people come to him declaring, 'Surely God is in you, and there is no other, no god besides him' (verse 14). One of the challenges of theology is that we just manage to squeeze God in a nice neat box and he leaps out and messes up all of our theories! I love that God is happy to call a guy who is not yet born, his anointed, then raise him up as a deliverer before he even knows who God is, and even to go on to make him a shadowy type of the ultimate Messiah, Jesus.

Let's pause and reflect . . .

1. Think about a priest as a mediator between God and humankind. Place yourself in that role and ask God to show you his heart for your community.
2. Now pray that back to God.
3. Now reflect on how that might affect your role at work/school/home/the gym/ballet lessons . . .
4. If you are not an intercessor in these contexts, who will be?
5. Is God raising up a Cyrus that you are aware of, for whom you could be praying right now?

16: Fatness

Apparently, two out of three people in the UK are now overweight. Fatness has become the big fat enemy as we all want to live longer and stay looking younger as long as possible. However, fatness has not always had such a bad press. Any student of art history will agree that the 21st-century aesthetic is a relatively recent preference. Chubby cherubs and lavishly thighed women graced the canvases adorning the walls of the fashionable elite in 1600s Europe. In many cultures fatness was seen as a sign of health and prosperity, whereas thinness was associated with poor diet and general poverty. The language of the Old Testament sometimes uses words like fatness to indicate the bountiful productiveness of the earth – prosperity and favour from God. There are words which are sometimes translated as fat or fatness which appear elsewhere translated as olive oil, or anointing.

Listen to Job describing his life before all of his famous trials set in:

Oh, for the days when I was in my prime,
 when God's intimate friendship blessed my house,

> *when the Almighty was still with me*
> *and my children were around me,*
> *when my path was drenched with cream*
> *and the rock poured out for me streams of olive oil.* (Job 29:4–6 NIV)

Notice, there's the Rock again (see chapter 1), he's there even with Job, in what is thought by some to be the earliest book of the Bible to be written. Job knew what it was like to be a friend of God. He knew what it felt like to be covered in the anointing and to enjoy the favour of an open heaven.

The beauty diet

Ezekiel is a book stuffed with prophetic visions and metaphors. Chapter 16 tells the story of an abandoned baby girl lying discarded in a field. This baby is unloved, dirty and dying, wallowing in her own blood, but God passes by, has compassion, and picks her up. We understand that the little girl is a metaphor for the city of Jerusalem. The prophet writes a very moving account of how God personally tends to her intimate care. She does not die, but rather begins to thrive. In verse 8, we read how God covers her naked body with the corner of his robe – this is the same picture of the legal redemption of a bride we see acted out in the story of Ruth. God enters into a covenant with her and she becomes his. Ezekiel paints a complex picture where we see God's relationship with the people he loves, first using the imagery of adoption, and then in the language of marriage – in fact, some of the vocabulary is identical to that of the great masterpiece of romantic poetry, The Song of Songs. This girl has morphed into a beautiful young woman, with whom God is clearly in love – I know, the ideas are intentionally provocative. Verse 9 describes how God bathes her, cleansing her from her blood, then anoints her with oil. If we cut and paste this story into the New Testament it contains all of the big themes of the gospel: redemption (being legally bought out of slavery), adoption, the bride of Christ, baptism in water and baptism in the Holy Spirit. Wow!

God not only clothes her, but gives her rare and expensive gifts: 'Thus you were adorned with gold and silver, and your clothing was of fine linen and silk and embroidered cloth. You ate fine flour and honey and oil. You grew exceedingly beautiful and advanced to royalty' (verse 13). Take a look at her diet: fine flour, honey and oil. If we unpack the metaphor, she is feeding on the finely ground wheat which was an option for a sin offering for poor people, along with the honey of revelation from the word of God and the oil of the anointing of the Holy Spirit. She is living on a diet of repentance, allowing God to purify her heart, along with the words from God's lips and the Christing of the Holy Spirit. No wonder she becomes so beautiful! The impact of this divinely given beauty was global – the nations of the world were impacted by her perfect loveliness.

This passage in the book of Ezekiel is a glimpse forwards to the culmination of God's desire for humanity to live in an exclusive covenant relationship with him as his bride. The Jerusalem spoken of by Ezekiel succeeded in breaking God's heart by her unfaithfulness to him, using her beauty and wealth to attract other lovers and go after other gods. The book of Revelation, however, gives us a picture of the *new Jerusalem* dressed as a bride prepared for her husband:

> *'Hallelujah!*
> *For the Lord our God*

> *the Almighty reigns.*
> *Let us rejoice and exult*
>   *and give him the glory,*
> *for the marriage of the Lamb has come,*
>   *and his Bride has made herself ready;*
> *it was granted her to clothe herself*
>   *with fine linen, bright and pure'* –
> *for the fine linen is the righteous deeds of the saints.*
> (Revelation 19:6–8)

and,

> *I saw the Holy City, the new Jerusalem, coming down out of heaven*
> *from God, prepared as a bride beautifully dressed for her husband.*
> *And I heard a loud voice from the throne saying, 'Look! God's dwell-*
> *ing place is now among the people, and he will dwell with them. They*
> *will be his people, and God himself will be with them and be their*
> *God.'* (Revelation 21:2,3 NIV)

This is a beauty capable of impressing God himself! I would like to propose, in this age of dieting fads, the ancient, but always new, Beauty Diet – get your inner beauty taken care of and watch your beauty impact the world!

Back to the brothers

Let's jump back, just for a second, to the story of Jacob and Esau. Jacob had been fleeing from his brother, Esau, because Esau wanted to kill him. Esau wanted to kill Jacob because he had successfully tricked him out of his legitimate inheritance.

Not only that, Jacob had deceived their ageing and almost blind father into giving him the blessing which should have rightly come to Esau, as the firstborn son. Esau was so enraged that the only way he could cheer himself up at all, was by thinking of different ways to murder his brother. To the modern mind, it might seem a little odd that Esau was so upset; surely the blessing was just a bunch of words from a frail old man?

See, the smell of my son
    is as the smell of a field that the LORD has blessed!
May God give you of the dew of heaven
    and of the fatness of the earth
    and plenty of grain and wine.
Let peoples serve you,
    and nations bow down to you.
Be lord over your brothers,
    and may your mother's sons bow down to you.
Cursed be everyone who curses you,
    and blessed be everyone who blesses you! (Genesis 27:27–29)

However, the ancient peoples understood well the power of blessing and cursing. Isaac knew that what he was doing in pronouncing those words over his son was invoking and somehow initiating God's direct intervention in this young man's life. It is worth reflecting that even though Jacob at this stage of his life was a cheat and a thief, he was the man who was soon to meet with God and be radically transformed. He was to have his name Jacob swapped by God for Israel. He was to give his name to the nation uniquely chosen by God – formed from his own direct descendants. This blessing from his elderly blind father became the defining blessing over the whole nation of Israel. Isaac blessed Jacob with the dew from heaven, which suggests the blessing of heaven coming down onto the earth, and the *fatness* of the earth – this Hebrew word *mashmân* can be used for fat, vigorous, a fertile place or olive oil. There is a rich sense of God's favour coming down from heaven and pouring fatness, anointing and productivity on the earth. It is exactly the same sense as the language conveys in Psalm 133:2,3 which pictures God's blessing as the anointing oil running over the High Priest and the dew of heaven (see chapter 14). Isaac blessed Jacob with an open heaven and the anointing poured on the land making it fruitful.

Esau clearly believed he had lost something very valuable in not receiving the blessing from his father. In fact, when he came to Isaac to legitimately claim what should have been his, the old man shook violently as he realised what he had done, whilst Esau cried out 'with a great and exceeding bitter cry' (Genesis 27:34 KJV). Sadly, all Isaac could do was to serve up the leftovers blessing – it actually sounds more like a curse:

> *Then Isaac his father answered and said to him:*
> > *'Behold, away from the fatness of the earth shall your dwelling be,*
> > > *and away from the dew of heaven on high.*
> > *By your sword you shall live,*
> > > *and you shall serve your brother;*
> > *but when you grow restless*
> > > *you shall break his yoke from your neck.'* (Genesis 27:39,40,
> emphasis added)

Away from the blessing of God and the anointing of the Holy Spirit on our lives we are forced to live by our sword – fighting for what we want, fighting for identity, recognition – fighting for survival. Sadly, it's not uncommon to see Christians living an Esau existence. Somehow, the enemy has managed to trick them out of the Father's blessing – they live with a restlessness inside or in hostility and opposition towards those who do live with God's favour on their lives.

Psalm 2 describes this hostility towards God's Anointed One. We will discuss this more fully in chapter 18.

Let's pause and reflect . . .

1. Have you ever blessed your children? (That's assuming you have some, if not, go to number 2.) Irrespective of their age, gather them together with your spouse and invite the Holy Spirit to help you, then speak a blessing over each one. Begin in the first person, '*I* bless you ....' Allow the words to come from deep in your heart. Let them be a creative mix of your hopes for that child mixed with faith that God is watching over the blessings coming out of your mouth to make them happen.

2. If you don't have children, bless your spouse, fiancé, boyfriend/girlfriend, friend, neighbour, random person at church, someone in the street – get good at blessing.

3. Bless your business, your boss, the NHS, the Prime Minister or President. Become a blessing pro. Bless your dog, your cat, your farm . . .

4. Have you tried the Beauty Diet? Are you feeling younger?

17: The Lord's Anointed

Opening batsman

Saul, as we have said, was God's choice as an opening batsman for the Israelite monarchy. We have also commented that he needed approval from people to make him feel like a success. Saul never learned to draw aside to find his approval from God as David, and then Jesus after him, did. There was nothing wrong with the anointing – David and Saul both received the same anointing – the problem was lying deep in Saul's own heart. The need for human approval is never satisfied, it is like lust – you get a bit of gratification, you need more.

David was exactly what Saul needed when his army was held in deadlock by the giant Goliath. He was just what Saul did not need afterwards, when social media was celebrating David and starting to overlook Saul. The song that went viral: 'Saul has slain his thousands, and David his tens of thousands', must have been somewhat irksome to Saul. The very oxygen of approval he needed to survive was going instead to this shepherd boy. David was God's provision to Saul, but Saul's

brokenness meant that he could never make room for him. In
the end Saul's envy of David became a murderous obsession,
which left David running for his life and living in a cave.

Fugitive

One day, Saul's spies told him that David the outlaw had been
spotted out in the wilderness of Engedi, so he took a band of
warriors with him to hunt him down. As the chase wore on Saul
slipped into a cave because he needed the bathroom. What he
didn't realise was that David and his merry men were deeper in
the cave hiding in the darkness, feeling not very merry. David's
fiercely loyal warriors naturally thought this was God's divine
appointment for David to rid himself of the guy who was
relentlessly hounding him and claim the throne in one simple
move. David's response, however, is surprising, and profound:

> *Then David arose and stealthily cut off a corner of Saul's robe. And*
> *afterward David's heart struck him, because he had cut off a corner*
> *of Saul's robe. He said to his men, 'The LORD forbid that I should*
> *do this thing to my lord, the LORD's anointed, to put out my hand*
> *against him, seeing he is the LORD's anointed.' So David persuaded*
> *his men with these words and did not permit them to attack Saul.*
> (1 Samuel 24:4–7)

Although he had not harmed the king, David was very quickly
convicted in his heart that even what he had done was an assault
on the one God had chosen and who was anointed with the
Holy Spirit. Saul had long since stopped being a godly king;
he had long since stopped living in the good of the anointing;
he was now just doing a job from an entirely human fleshly

motivation – clinging to power. In spite of all of this, David himself was a spiritual man who understood the heavenly protocol surrounding the anointed servant of God. When Saul, in due course, died, David succeeded him as king, but his own hands were clean from trying to muscle God's plan into coming about according to his humanly preferred timescale.

Honouring the anointing

David knew how to honour the anointing. David honoured Saul and treated him with the respect he would give to a godly king. Saul, in spite of his brooding resentment towards the younger man, in turn, rose to the occasion, responded in a manner befitting a king, and blessed David. He prophesied that David would indeed succeed him as king: 'So may the LORD reward you with good for what you have done to me this day. And now, behold, I know that you shall surely be king, and that the kingdom of Israel shall be established in your hand' (1 Samuel 24:19,20). If we show honour to the anointed servants of God, even if they have been behaving poorly, we hand them an opportunity to return to their true identity.

When Saul did die, he was defeated in battle. He died as a king leading his people. Although this was David's big moment, not one tiniest hint of rejoicing was found in his heart. In fact, he and all his men tore their clothes, wept and fasted until the evening. He went on to compose a beautiful lament over the death of Saul and his son Jonathan which is now a piece of classic literature:

Saul and Jonathan, beloved and lovely!
  In life and in death they were not divided;

they were swifter than eagles;
    they were stronger than lions.
You daughters of Israel, weep over Saul,
    who clothed you luxuriously in scarlet,
    who put ornaments of gold on your apparel. (2 Samuel 1:23,24)

Superman, or Clark Kent

We should never try to excuse the inexcusable, but it is so important to rightly honour those whom God has called and seen fit to anoint with his Holy Spirit. Some of my favourite people in the Old Testament narrative are those we get to see epically fail. A classic example is Samson. Samson lived in the times before Israel had a king. God raised up successive leaders, or judges, to lead the nation – often whose primary job was to rescue the people from a powerful enemy. In Samson's day the trouble was coming in the form of relentless oppression from the neighbouring Philistines.

Samson grew up with a special call from God on his life from before he was born. He was truly a miracle baby – his mother had been unable to conceive, but then received a surprise visit from an angel who announced to her that she would become pregnant with a son. This baby even came with his own special care instructions – he was to be considered a Nazirite from birth. In the Old Testament a man or woman could choose to take a Nazirite vow for a period of time as a special way of devoting themselves to God. The person taking such a vow would then take on certain dietary restrictions, such as no alcoholic drinks and no grapes or raisins, whilst also stopping having haircuts or shaving for the period of the vow.[1] Samson was chosen from conception to be especially holy and set part for God in the same way John the Baptist would be, many years later.

As Samson grew he learned about his specialness: that he was not to have his hair cut, drink wine or go near dead bodies, including relatives. He also began to experience the anointing of the Holy Spirit flowing and surging upon him. 'And the young man grew, and the LORD blessed him. And the Spirit of the LORD began to stir him in Mahaneh-dan, between Zorah and Eshtaol' (Judges 13:24,25). He began to sense the Holy Spirit stirring up within him when he found himself in the Philistine held areas – he was beginning to sense why God had particularly called him and anointed him.

No Sunday school teacher

Samson was unconventional. If he lived in the UK today, he would probably not be given a job teaching in the Sunday school – he would certainly fail his safeguarding checks. The first time we read of his legendary strength he is making a journey on foot when he is attacked by a lion. He grabs the lion and slays it using only his bare hands. As a child, I had a Bible storybook with a picture of Samson looking like a bodybuilder

dead lion

with bulging muscles; however, he may have looked just like a regular guy with lots of hair. Shortly after the lion incident Samson picked up the jawbone of a dead donkey (evidently pushing the boundaries of his Nazirite status) and single-handedly took on 1,000 Philistine men, slaughtering them all.

Superficially, the account of Samson's life reads like a catalogue of chaotic, even foolish romances and random outbursts of rage resulting in spikes in the Philistine death rate. Reading a little more closely it's hard not to see an emotionally vulnerable man with a supernatural gift that is far bigger than he is. He successfully led the people of Israel for twenty years, but we tend to hear far more preaching about his failings than his successes. In spite of the mistakes God was clearly not far from him. For example, after his Jawbone Hill victory he was thirsty, so cried out to the Lord:

> *Because he was very thirsty, he cried out to the LORD, 'You have given your servant this great victory. Must I now die of thirst and fall into the hands of the uncircumcised?' Then God opened up the hollow place in Lehi, and water came out of it. When Samson drank, his strength returned and he revived. So the spring was called En Hakkore, and it is still there in Lehi.* (Judges 15:18,19 NIV)

God's flaky friends

God performs the very miracle he had for Moses, for Samson – producing water from the Rock. Even in the crazy chaos of the life of a man ruled by his passions, Jesus the Rock is present flowing with life-giving water. God loves his friends, even the ropey, unreliable ones like me! He shows remarkable loyalty to those he calls, even though we sometimes fail and even bring dishonour to his name. I still cannot get my head around the fact that Jesus – in heaven, with the Father and the angels – is called the Son of David, or even the Lion of the Tribe of Judah! David was a great guy, but he was also an adulterer and a very calculated murderer. Judah, meanwhile, had sex with his own daughter-in-law! His excuse was that he thought she was a prostitute – umm! Nonetheless, in the book of Revelation we read that the gates of the heavenly city are named after the twelve tribes of Israel – a pretty motley crew! Meanwhile the foundation stones of the city are named after the twelve first apostles of Jesus, his friends.

The point I am trying to make is not that we should live carelessly, or excuse sin in people just because they are called by God, but rather that we should recognise and give honour to those God has graced with his holy anointing. Jesus himself said that if we recognise a prophet as a prophet, we receive the reward a prophet brings – direction, inspiration, encouragement, comfort and confirmation (Matthew 10:41). Jesus, the only perfect prophet, was fully aware of the flawed nature of men and women, even the ones God has called to a significant task. When we honour the Christed servant we are honouring the anointing. When we honour the anointing, we are honouring the person of the Holy Spirit.

(No lions were injured making this book.)

Let's pause and reflect . . .

1. Have you ever been disappointed by a man or woman in leadership whom you were initially drawn to because of the evidence of the anointing on them?
2. How can you 'process' the feeling of disappointment without judging or dishonouring the Holy Spirit? (Take a look at our process of forgiveness at the end of chapter 4.)
3. Think about the celebrity culture. Why do you think we put prominent Christian leaders on pedestals?
4. Think about the difference between the Marvel Comic superhero concept alongside the regular human being clothed in the supernatural anointing of the Holy Spirit.
5. How do we encourage people into Christian ministry/politics/business/entertainment, cheering them on, and at the same time help them to handle success and a raised profile?
6. Is there any way back for a fallen hero like Samson?

18: Anti Christ

Dead flies and fake anointing

Solomon, the writer of the book of Ecclesiastes, was responsible for the phrase which is still in use today, *a fly in the ointment*. He wrote: 'Dead flies make the perfumer's ointment give off a stench; so a little folly outweighs wisdom and honour' (Ecclesiastes 10:1). An exclusive fragrant lotion crafted by one of

dead flies in the ointment

the finest perfumers in the world to emphasise one's beauty can be made to stink by the decomposing remains of a fly. So, too, we can pollute the anointing of the Holy Spirit by ministering with rotting dead bits of flesh in the mix. In the first book of Samuel, we discover how the sons of Eli were anointed as priests, but their lives were so displeasing to God that he brought a swift judgement, bringing their lives and their ministries to an untimely end.

Tragic are the stories of men and women who were once filled with the Holy Spirit, entrusted with the rare and costly oil reserved for kings and priests – Christed ones indeed – but who held on to their own vanity, greed or lust whilst continuing to operate in ministry. Instead of spreading the fragrance of Christ everywhere, they spread the stench of decomposition. Their legacy has been ultimately to dishonour that glorious name.

It is normal for us to long to see God move – it is desirable that we should cry out to God to move through us. It is even legitimate for us to look at men and women of God and wish to be like them in their effectiveness in ministry. Paul teaches that we should imitate the lives of men and women who walk with God. It is possible, however, for us also to covet the apparent trappings of success – visibility, wealth and popularity – because of our own need for recognition and significance. The world desperately needs anointed ones; in fact, the whole of creation is groaning waiting for them. It is waiting for those who are true sons and daughters, who know they are loved and valued by the Father. Such sons and daughters are no longer orphans in need of approval – they have experienced the embrace of the Father.

I always hate the part in a movie where everything starts to go wrong: the good guy looks like he's really the bad guy, and the bad guy looks set to hijack the whole story. I hate it even more when I read that false christs will appear and succeed in deceiving people. It would be great to be able to dismiss such things as scaremongering and conspiracy theory, yet the warnings in the Bible are clear, and some are from Jesus himself. Jesus gives a sober warning about false christs in his famous speech about the times and events leading up to his return and the end of the world. He indicates that certain people will arise on the earth endowed with supernatural ability to perform powerful signs and wonders which seem to authenticate them as having been sent from God. The context he describes is a time of intense distress on the earth, where people will be looking for some kind of hope and relief from the suffering (see Matthew 24:24).

Paul also prophesies about a period of time in the countdown to the end of the world, referring to it as 'the rebellion' (2 Thessalonians 2). He describes a *man of lawlessness* who is armed with the ability to perform false miracles, enabling him to powerfully delude many people. According to Paul, this man's arrival on the world stage will be consistent with the works of Satan – Jesus described Satan as a murderer and a liar, indeed the father of lies.

> *The coming of the lawless one will be in accordance with how Satan works. He will use all sorts of displays of power through signs and wonders that serve the lie, and all the ways that wickedness deceives those who are perishing. They perish because they refused to love the truth and so be saved. For this reason God sends them a powerful delusion so that they will believe the lie and so that all will be condemned who have not believed the truth but have delighted in wickedness.* (2 Thessalonians 2:9–12 NIV)

Modern history presents a grisly body of evidence, that given the right social and economic conditions, rational, educated people can make shocking choices and follow the most hideously evil leaders. The list of leaders of nations who have come 'in accordance with the work of Satan' must include Adolf Hitler, Josef Stalin, Pol Pot, Idi Amin, and many others. These men, however evil, seem to have relied largely on rhetoric and sheer brutality to influence people. The Man of Lawlessness identified by Jesus and Paul will have supernatural influence as well. It seems clear that the people who will be deceived by the Man of Lawlessness, or the antichrist, are those who have already refused to love the truth (verse 10). Those who are drawn to power, but have never fallen in love with Jesus, are always vulnerable to being enticed into compromise. The true anointing from God flows from intimate encounters with him. The more we become intimate with him – the more our hearts become aligned with his – the more readily we sense when something is from a different spirit or an unclean source.

Fake christs

The purpose of creating a counterfeit of anything is to obtain a high price in exchange for something relatively cheap, even worthless. Works of art, electronic gadgets, designer clothing, bank notes – the production of fake goods and money is big business. Counterfeiters usually imitate items with a high value. They are therefore more interested in high-denomination notes than the copper coins which hide in sofas and under car seats. It is not surprising, then, that the deceiver goes to extreme lengths to counterfeit something as priceless as the anointing. Jesus, the Anointed One, is the most precious of all. His Christing sets captives free and raises those who are dead to life. He brings hope to the hopeless.

Western society at present seems split into two camps: the cynical, rational mind which flatly refuses to believe in anything supernatural, and the more mystical mind that is interested in anything 'spiritual' as long as it does not challenge my lifestyle.

Then if anyone says to you, 'Look, here is the Christ!' or 'There he is!' do not believe it. For false christs and false prophets will arise and perform great signs and wonders, so as to lead astray, if possible, even the elect. See, I have told you beforehand. So, if they say to you, 'Look, he is in the wilderness', do not go out. If they say, 'Look, he is in the inner rooms', do not believe it. For as the lightning comes from the east and shines as far as the west, so will be the coming of the Son of Man. Wherever the corpse is, there the vultures will gather. (Matthew 24:23–28)

In his first letter, the apostle John makes it pretty clear that the spirit of antichrist is already out and about on the earth. He defines any spirit or way of thinking which denies that Jesus is the Christ as the spirit of antichrist. It is an earthly mindset which refuses to receive the revelation from the Father of whom the Son is. *Anti* means before, against or instead of. The spirit of antichrist is a demonic spirit which gives rise to a cultural mindset opposed to the genuine anointing. It denies the work of the Holy Spirit – it opposes the Christed One (Jesus) and the Christed ones (you and me). It is the mindset which elevates human achievement as most important; it is a dark satanic lie which lurks in every strand of Western culture, including much of the church. Psalm 115:4 describes idolatry as the worship of 'the work of human hands'. It is the worship of what we have created, by ourselves. The spirit of antichrist is illustrated in the famous second psalm:

Why do the nations rage
and the peoples plot in vain?
The kings of the earth set themselves,
and the rulers take counsel together,
*against the L*ord *and against his Anointed, saying,*
'Let us burst their bonds apart
and cast away their cords from us.' (Psalm 2:1–3)

Look at this hostility towards the Lord's Anointed One! The human mind sees coming under the lordship of Jesus as something restrictive – something to resist and fight against, in the same way that Esau did not want to come under the leadership of his brother, Jacob. The apostle John writes: 'Who is the liar? It is whoever denies that Jesus is the Christ. Such a person is the antichrist – denying the Father and the Son. No one who denies the Son has the Father; whoever acknowledges the Son has the Father also' (1 John 2:22,23 NIV).

Who do people say that I am?

Jesus asked his disciples what the word on the street was as to his real identity. They reported that some thought he was John the Baptist returned to life, others thought he was Elijah, while still others thought Jeremiah, or one of the prophets. He then made it personal – 'But who do you say that I am?' It should be pointed out that Jesus was not suddenly suffering from a moment of insecurity, rather he wanted to hear his students make the confession. The disciples were silent, but outspoken Peter was in no doubt whatsoever and declared, 'You are the Christ, the Son of the living God' (Matthew 16:14–16). Jesus was super-excited by this answer and said that Peter had not reached this conclusion as a result of his amazing powers of deduction, but had actually received revelation from God. You are the Messiah, the Anointed Son of God, was an answer that could not be worked out by human reasoning.

A.W. Tozer, the great prophetic preacher commented: 'I remind you that there are churches so completely out of the hands of God that if the Holy Spirit withdrew from them, they wouldn't find it out for many months.'[1] In church programmes and planning there is a huge reliance on things making sense. There is a kind of popular churchy wisdom which goes along the lines of, 'God gave us brains, so we should use them.' Well, of course that is true, but if Jesus is to build his church, we also need to be attentive to his voice and obedient when he speaks. Jesus may well require us to do things which don't make sense to us at the time. I doubt very much that Ananias could see any sense whatsoever in going to visit the man called Saul, who a couple days before had been authorised to round up Christians and put them in chains. However, God spoke to him and he obeyed. God healed Saul's eyes and he went on to become Paul, the great apostle to the Gentiles. It's interesting to note that even though Paul had a God-ordained, God-delivered conversion, he still needed the hands of a human being laid on him in order to receive the Holy Spirit.

The elevation of human reason above the voice of God is to succumb to the hypnotic spirit of antichrist. This spirit, or demonically conceived mindset of anti-anointing is as busy in the church today as it has always been. In the UK in recent years, fear has been given a place of major influence in society and it has set up camp in church too. We write business plans and risk assessments, create policies and take out insurances, just in case. We ask God to bless our plans, but how much time is spent asking God for his plans? Do you remember we said earlier, that God never asks us to do things we could do by ourselves without his supernatural help.

Yeah, well how do we know it's God?

I have been in meetings (not many, thankfully) where the idea of being led by the Holy Spirit is subtly mocked, as if it is a poor second to good planning. The problem appears to be that not all Christian leaders are skilled or practised in hearing God's voice, so have no real confidence that listening to God would actually get us anywhere – I guess they imagine it means sitting around gazing at our belly buttons. However, in the early days of the church the leaders fully expected God to speak. 'While they were worshipping the Lord and fasting, the Holy Spirit said, "Set apart for me Barnabas and Saul for the work to which I have called them." Then after fasting and praying they laid their hands on them and sent them off' (Acts 13:2,3).

These disciples were worshipping God and fasting – we call it waiting on God – and he spoke. Normal. Very cool, but very normal! To the disciples, the Holy Spirit was a person notice-ably present in the room. This prayer meeting was actually to be a major turning point in the development of the church. It was the official launch of the apostolic ministry of Paul and Barnabas to the Gentiles, which turns out to be very good news for me, as I am a Gentile. It's interesting to notice that the Holy Spirit says, 'for the work to which I have called them'. The Holy Spirit, the person who is the anointing, has plans for you and me and for the church. From this point on, Paul always refers to himself as an apostle of Jesus Christ, by the will of God. There is no ambiguity – the apostles were very familiar with the voice of the Holy Spirit, because he sounds like Jesus. They rec-ognised the voice of the Holy Spirit as the voice of God.

Later on, the first generation of apostles were meeting to dis-cuss business in relation to the emerging Gentile church. Most of these apostles were Jewish, so they had a culture and customs foreign to the Gentile Christians, including the practice of cir-cumcision. Various senior leaders stood up and presented their sense of what the Holy Spirit was saying, then the assembled group made a decision which they put into a letter. The way they phrased it shows a picture of grown men with perfectly good functioning brains submitting their cultural preferences to the voice of the senior Senior Partner: 'For it has seemed good to the Holy Spirit and to us to lay on you no greater burden than these requirements' (Acts 15:28). They knew how to listen to the Holy Spirit and make decisions under the anointing of his presence.

A.W. Tozer summed it up perfectly: 'I want the presence of God Himself, or I don't want anything at all to do with religion . . . I want all that God has or I don't want any.'[2]

Yep, me too!

Let's pause and reflect . . .

1. What might be the best way to avoid 'dead flies' contaminating the anointing?
2. How do we deal with our own natural ambition to succeed – and is that a bad desire?
3. What place do you give to hearing from God in your planning?
   - For your own future
   - For the future of your family
   - For the future of your church/ministry project
   - For the future of your business
4. Can you identify those moments when the Holy Spirit seems to strongly endorse a particular train of thought in a conversation, or a suggested solution to a problem?
5. Do you recognise a sense of the Holy Spirit saying 'no' in certain instances?

A prayer about success:

Thank you, Lord, that you did not call me to lead me into failure. Thank you that you have taken me from my past failings, lifted me up and seated me with princes. Thank you that the highest aim I could possibly have is to live my life as a gift to you, who has given me everything, and taken away all of my shame. I surrender all of my hopes, dreams, aspirations and ambitions to you. You know about each of my preferences, and I now put them down at your feet. I know that you love me. I believe your plans are to prosper me and not to harm me, so as I move forward in my call to ………………… I trust that you will keep me daily aware of the fact that my success comes from you. I trust you to walk with me into whatever context in which I find myself as a result of following the opportunities you place before me. Thank you that promotion comes from you. Let me wear success well.

19: Raising Young Messiahs

Basket case

Sometimes, I wish God would boom from the heavens, like write something really big across the night sky, or do something so massive that everyone can see at once and believe in him – job done! However, his plan is so often sneaky – completely under the radar and completely open to misinterpretation. The cool thing, though, is that he always leaves a trail of breadcrumbs for the prophets to pick up. Jesus' birth is the classic example – he sends an angel to a young teenage girl in a village. She has a distant connection to noble ancestry, traceable to King David, but otherwise she's a nobody. The angel tells her that she's going to become supernaturally pregnant with God's baby. This is so open to misinterpretation, even a relatively trusting person would be somewhat suspicious of such a story. God's master plan to save the universe was to send a baby.

It's a baby Messiah.

So many times when the situation was desperate, God's answer was not to send an army, or even a superhero, but a baby! Israel was a nation in slavery – it was approaching 400 years of grinding misery when a baby is born to a mum and dad, who themselves are slaves. The Bible records that they saw he was 'no ordinary child' (Acts 7:20; Hebrews 11:23). Surely, almost every new parent ever looks at their child and sees something special. Most of us parents believe our own child to be the most beautiful child ever born, and probably the most intelligent alive – that is, at least until they can disagree with us! In the tiny Moses, his mum and dad recognised something which I'm sure was the anointing, and so concocted one of the most crazy plans ever conceived: a little floating cradle made of twigs. I think God was smiling to himself and chuckling to the angels at the sheer fragility of this escape plan for his precious people group.

At the very best, all we parents can hope to give our young messiahs, to fully safeguard them from the evil Pharaoh who wants to

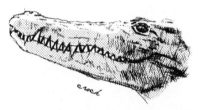

feed them to the crocodiles, is a floating basket of twigs. We come up with great plans, set good boundaries, pray our heads off, but it's God who writes the story. How beautiful, but how delicate, the woven wicker lifeboat carrying the mini-messiah, conducted by the current of the Nile to the bathing princess. Her heart is melted by the plight of the one solitary Hebrew baby, whilst her father's heart is flinty and unmoved by the humanitarian crisis he has brought upon the whole Hebrew nation. The capacity of the princess to open her heart to the baby Moses, sets the scene for this young messiah to grow up in the house of Pharaoh, whilst observing first-hand the sufferings of his people.

Care instructions

Let's quickly return to the story of Samson. When the angel visited the wife of Manoah and told her that she was to have a child, as we have said, he went on to give her very specific instructions about how this son was to be raised. During the pregnancy she must abstain from alcohol and from eating any food which was unclean, that is, forbidden under the food laws given to the Jewish people by Moses. She was told that the boy she was to bear was a special child and would be set apart for a very holy purpose, even from his birth. He was not to have a razor used on his head; he must never have a haircut, nor was he permitted to eat grapes, raisins or drink alcohol. He was to be a Nazirite. On the one hand, the Nazirite was a very special person; on the other hand, any man or woman could choose to take the vow to belong to God in this unique way. Besides avoiding alcohol, grapes and raisins, the vow involved steering well clear of dead people, even close relatives. The Nazirite was a prophetic sign to the nation of Israel. To see a man or woman who was willing to voluntarily put God first in their own life, simply because he or she saw the reward in being personally close to him, was a challenge to others and to the nation to raise their game.

Famous Nazirites besides Samson include the prophet Samuel and John the Baptist. Each of these guys had quite unique upbringings: Samson never had his hair cut or ate any food or drink derived from grapes; Samuel also was exempted from the barbers, and from early childhood he was brought to live at Shiloh, the place where the people came to sacrifice to God before the temple was built. His mother's promise to God was, 'As soon as the child is weaned, I will bring him, so that he may

appear in the presence of the LORD and dwell there for ever'
(1 Samuel 1:22) and, 'For this child I prayed, and the LORD
has granted me my petition that I made to him. Therefore I
have lent him to the LORD. As long as he lives, he is lent to the
LORD' (1 Samuel 1:27,28).

Imagine, lending your child to the Lord for as long as he or she
lives! Amazingly, the young Samuel didn't rebel against the life
his mother chose for him, but from early years developed the
ability to listen to God's voice with pinpoint accuracy. In fact,
his prophecies were so spot-on that the Bible says, 'And Samuel
grew, and the LORD was with him and let none of his words fall
to the ground' (1 Samuel 3:19).

I believe that right now God is calling young people and children into a lifestyle where they have chosen to make him the
first thing in their lives. They are instinctively looking for
something which will cost them. They are not attracted by
the vanity of acquiring titles and stuff, but do want to change
the world. They are the young messiahs; the Christed ones – the
sons of God that the creation is groaning for. Babies are being
born today who are not ordinary children – they are part of
God's answer to a world that doesn't know him. We parents are
so crucial in this process; we can cooperate with, or hinder the
plans of heaven for the young people growing up in our homes.
That is why Samson's mum and dad received the care instructions from the angel. That's why John the Baptist's dad was not
able to speak until he was completely onboard with God's purpose for his son's life. As parents we can fulfil Hannah's desire
for her son – that he may appear in the presence of the Lord
and dwell there forever. We must create the atmosphere in our
home where the young messiah learns to recognise the presence

of God, and where they learn how to identify the voice of God amongst all the other voices competing for their attention.

Rejecting the sweet in favour of the sweetest

I would imagine there were times when the young John the Baptist fancied some of the grapes on the table and mum had to swipe the fruit bowl from his reach. It may be that Elizabeth and Zechariah decided that they would completely abstain from alcohol to make the home environment an easier place for the teenage John to manage. Sometimes the young person may not welcome the reminder from mum or dad that they have a destiny from God to fulfil. Samson appears to have been irritated by the wish of his parents that he should marry a nice Jewish girl, and intentionally went looking for someone a little more exotic – a Philistine. A Nazirite man or woman was noticeably different from their peers, they stood out from the crowd. With their long hair and the men with their free-range beards, they did look a bit weird! So also young people who choose to wait until marriage to begin a sexual relationship look very different from their contemporaries. They, like the Nazirite, become a source of ridicule as well as a provocation to holiness. I will never forget the amusement of two married guys I was working with on a building site when they discovered that I had waited until I was married. After about twenty minutes of comedy at my expense they settled down and one said, 'Actually, man, I really respect that.' The other one chipped in, 'Yeah, I wish I had waited – you just get to the same shallow point of relationship with every girl, and you never get to really know them.' Then more laughing as they admitted there was no chance they would have succeeded.

John the Baptist lived a lifestyle separated to God. As he became a man he spent his time alone with God, living in the wild places. Although his diet excluded anything to do with grapes (the legal sweet of the health police) he lived on honey, which is even sweeter. He abstained from the sweet to enjoy the sweetest. He chose to avoid the obvious and instant pleasures of this life to grow close to God and to make him his greatest pleasure. Fasting is when we abstain from legitimate pleasures such as food to find the deepest pleasure of true intimacy with God. During a two-week fast at the Prayerhouse, I was so thrilled to be told that each young person in the youth group was fasting from food – either missing a meal a day, or fasting for the weekend. One teenage girl said that she had seen her dad fasting for the first week and wanted to join with what he was doing. The same happened with my two teenage daughters. I love that these girls saw their dads fasting. The dads were setting the spiritual thermostat in the home for the raising of young messiahs.

As Christmas approached, a couple of guys and I were reflecting that the one area of Jesus' life we would like to know more about was his childhood and youth. Luke tells us that he 'grew and became strong, filled with wisdom. And the favour of God was upon him' (Luke 2:40). This is awesome, but we have to resort to guesswork as to what that really looked like – we don't get much more until the time he gets left behind in Jerusalem. However, it's a pretty good clue – he was growing up as a human boy, but even during this fraught process he stood out because the hand of God was visibly upon him. I would love to know how he coped when the cute little girl from the village caught his eye and transmitted that most magical of messages with her eyes: 'I'm interested in you . . .' I would love to know how he handled watered-down faith at the Rabbinical school, or the annoying customer who wanted him to completely modify the carpentry job he had spent a week making without adding to the price.

Where's that boy gone . . . ?

Mary and Joseph were no doubt doing a fab job of fostering the Christing in the life of Jesus, right up until the time of his first miracle, but really they were playing catch-up a fair bit of the time. On occasions, our young messiah may have a clearer insight into what they need than we do at a particular time. Mary and Joseph had a pattern of going up to Jerusalem once a year to celebrate the Passover festival. It seems that Joseph took some time off work and a crowd from the village all headed to the capital together, on a kind of pilgrimage. Everyone knew everyone, so it was a great environment for the young people – they could hang out together without needing parental micro-management. This was fine, until they were on their way home again and Mary realised she hadn't seen her son lately. Most parents will recognise the hot, panicky, guilty feeling of, 'Oh no!' followed by the frantic interrogation of the entire group, 'When did you last see him?' and, 'I thought he was with you, Joseph . . .' Guilt-tripping, brain-racking and step-retracing (wishing someone would hurry up and invent the smartphone), the Nazareth group all return to Jerusalem and arrive once more at the Temple, three days after they first left. Relief and frustration follow in quick succession as they recognise the Holy Boy, sitting locked deep in conversation with the top biblical scholars and teachers of the day. Jesus may have been the actual Messiah, but at that moment he was the just-found, had-been-missing twelve-year-old.

I'm not quite sure how well mum and dad received his explanation, 'Didn't you realise that I must be busy with my dad's business?' (Luke 2:49, my paraphrase).

Mary was smart and wise; she treasured these memories in her heart, often reflecting on them and putting them together with the words of the angel, memories of the visit and gifts of the Magi along with bits of scripture and prophecies which she remembered and the words from Simeon and Anna at the Temple.

A sword will pierce you

When Simeon prophesied over Mary and Joseph as they presented Jesus at the Temple, about her part in God's plan, he gave her a warning: 'and a sword will pierce through your own soul also' (Luke 2:35). It can be a bittersweet assignment, being called to raise a young messiah. We know that dear Mary was on her knees weeping as her beloved son was hoisted up in front of the jeering mob – wincing as she watched his bones wrenched out of joint as the cross jolted into the hole in the ground. She had nursed this holy boy at her own breast, kissed his sweaty head as he nestled in to her bosom, and watched with pride as her firstborn had taught the multitudes and healed the sick. Now, she knew he must be taken from her. She knew, more than anyone else, how undeserving of the shame of the criminal execution this young man was – how unfair the brutal lashes, the merciless mocking and spitting of the thugs paid to snuff out his life. She had lived in the atmosphere of heaven that Jesus had brought into her home for thirty-three years. She had looked into those eyes that bore her own DNA, yet the one looking back at her was God himself.

Now, centuries on, we can see just how and why all generations have indeed called her blessed.[1] At the time of the young Jesus, she was just a mum, changing diapers, teaching her son to walk, helping him learn the scriptures and imparting a deep sense of identity. May God raise up in the 21st century the mums and dads who will co-operate with the Spirit of God in raising young messiahs, Christed to preach good news to a world that is groaning in waiting.

laid on the nail

Let's pause and reflect . . .

1. What can be done to help raise young messiahs by those of us who have no children?
2. What about the oldies? Are they out of the story?
3. What steps can you take to create an environment where your young person can discover how to live in the Christing?
4. Adopt a school. Take on a local school as a prayer project. Invest yourself: if you are able to, maybe volunteer to regularly hear children read, or become a school governor.

20: Reaching a Conclusion

Demolishing Hades

We have already mentioned the story recorded by Matthew, Mark and Luke as they describe the moment at Caesarea Philippi where Jesus asks his disciples who they think he is. Each writer records Peter's response: 'You are the Christ.' In Matthew's account of this moment, Jesus commends Peter:

> *And Jesus answered him, 'Blessed are you, Simon Bar-Jonah! For flesh and blood has not revealed this to you, but my Father who is in heaven. And I tell you, you are Peter, and on this rock I will build my church, and the gates of hell shall not prevail against it. I will give you the keys of the kingdom of heaven, and whatever you bind on earth shall be bound in heaven, and whatever you loose on earth shall be loosed in heaven.' Then he strictly charged the disciples to tell no one that he was the Christ.* (Matthew 16:17–20)

This is one of those loaded passages of the New Testament which has launched doctrines, sparked controversies and fuelled a million sermons, and to which I will now have the audacity to add my comments! The region of Caesarea Philippi was famous for the worship of various Greek and pagan deities. Today, the area known as Banias, or Panias, is a historical site where archaeological evidence points to the worship of Pan, among others. It was known as the Gates of Hades because of the depraved rituals involving goats that were conducted there.

Earlier in this book we have seen how the Anointed One is sometimes identified as a rock, or even possibly manifests as a rock. Now, in these densely significant few verses of scripture we hear Peter name Jesus as 'The Christ, the Son of the Living God'. Jesus, clearly playing with words, says, 'Bingo! Well done, Simon, son of Jonah, ten out of ten! This is not a piece of smart human deduction, but a revelation from God. You are now Peter . . .' (my paraphrase). Let's pause. The name Simon means 'he has heard', Peter means 'rock', or 'stone'. We named our son Joshua because it comes from the Hebrew name Yeshua, which, translated into the New Testament Greek, is Jesus. He's not *the* Jesus, but we could say that he is a Jesus. Let me be bold; Peter was not *the* Rock, but he was a rock. Jesus is *the* Rock. Peter was, and still is, a towering foundation stone of the church. We owe him so much, along with all of the apostles and martyrs of our faith. Paul says that the church is built upon the foundation of apostles and prophets (Ephesians 2:20), but he also strenuously contended, there is only one Foundation, that is Jesus Christ – the Anointed Rock (1 Corinthians 3:11).

Jesus was saying, 'Simon, *he has heard* (from heaven); you too are a *rock* (Peter), like I am the Rock. The Christ you have so rightly identified is the Rock on whom the church is built, he will demolish the very gates of Hades with all the disgusting trappings you can see all around us.' To those today who also correctly see Jesus as the Christ, he is still saying the same thing: 'You too are anointed – Christed – you too are a rock on which is built the church, the *Ekklesia*, the called-out Hades Gates demolition crew.'

Stay with this thought just a little longer. According to Mark, six days later Jesus took Peter, James and John on a hike up a high mountain. Traditionally this 'high mountain' has been taken to be Mount Tabor. Many scholars now think it is more likely to have been Mount Hermon, which is relatively near to Caesarea Philippi. Whilst they are together in that remote spot, observing the view and talking with Jesus, the three disciples are suddenly aware that they have company. Moses and Elijah have joined the summit meeting. (We have briefly mentioned this occasion before in chapter 12.) Moses is seen by theologians as the lawgiver – he received the Ten Commandments on the stone tablets and established the rule of God's law in the fledgling nation of Israel, whilst Elijah is seen as the archetypal prophet of the Old Testament era. On the top of this mountain, we see Jesus, the Anointed One, having a meeting with the Law and the Prophets. Here is the most Holy Spirit-centred individual who ever walked the earth coming together with the Law and the Prophets on Mount Hermon, whilst the visible glory of God covers him. Here is Psalm 133 again, this time from The Passion Translation:

How truly wonderful and delightful
to see brothers and sisters living together in sweet unity!
It's as precious as the sacred scented oil
flowing from the head of the high priest Aaron,
dripping down upon his beard and running all the way down
to the hem of his priestly robes.
This heavenly harmony can be compared to the dew
dripping down from the skies upon Mount Hermon,
refreshing the mountain slopes of Israel.
For from this realm of sweet harmony
God will release his eternal blessing, the promise of life forever!
(Psalm 133 TPT)

Jesus is the point where the Torah (Law) and the Prophets meet in perfect unity with the Holy Spirit. Later, after his resurrection as he walked with two other grieving disciples, he took them on a guided tour of the Old Testament scriptures. 'And beginning with Moses and all the Prophets, he interpreted to them in all the Scriptures the things concerning himself' (Luke 24:27).

Plain sight

For centuries the Jewish people were the custodians of the scriptures. They did a fantastic job of preserving them intact for future generations, including you and me. Their obsession with accuracy meant that each handwritten copy of the scripture that was made was identical to the one copied from. However, although they devoted zillions of hours studying the words, even including the punctuation, they didn't really get the idea of the Messiah – the Anointed or Christed One. Their cultural spectacles didn't work like our scuba mask in chapter 1, but worked more like frosted glass, keeping Jesus obscured. All of the details of the law, the priests, sacrifices and festivals point to the Messiah: Jesus. The kaleidoscopic mosaic of prophetic visions and words all point to our glorious heaven-opener. They also point to the outrageously exalted place that God has reserved in the grand story for *people*. The Jewish scholars could only think in terms of an earthly kingdom like Israel under the rule of David. 'You search the Scriptures because you think that in them you have eternal life; and it is they that bear witness about me' (John 5:39). Jesus the Messiah was on every page, hidden in plain sight.

Just as the Messiah was hidden in plain sight throughout the Old Testament scriptures, so, too, the anointing of the Holy Spirit is entirely central to the scripture and our understanding of Jesus and the ministry he entrusted to his church, yet easily missed. The awesome revelation of the anointing should not be monopolised by, or portrayed as the preserve of any particular brand or denomination. Within Christian theology there has always been a spectrum of belief ranging from a very deterministic emphasis, where God's will for each of us is predestined – mapped out for us even before we were born, through to an almost opposite view which depends much more on the choices made by the exercise of free will of the individual. My sincere hope is that our journey together has illustrated the dynamic interplay between the Sovereign God and the fully autonomous, deeply loved human children which is made possible by the anointing of the Holy Spirit.

Bringing it all together

Three human apostles, friends of Jesus, had been invited into this extraordinary meeting on the mountain with the Christed One, plus the Lawgiver and Prophet. They are terrified and say irrelevant things, even falling asleep during the meeting, but there they are. They are personally invited into an open-heaven moment. The dazzlingly bright glory of God covers Jesus, and a cloud – remember the cloud – covers them, as the Father booms from heaven, directing the mortals to listen to his Beloved Son. 'And suddenly, looking around, they no longer saw anyone with them but Jesus only' (Mark 9:8). We began our journey by considering the story of Jacob the fugitive and his experience of the heavens opened at Bethel. Here, on the mountain in this moment of transfiguration, it all comes together again. Human beings representing the newly launched church, or *Ekklesia* – God's special called-out ones – are brought together with the Law, Prophets, and the glory of God at the invitation of Jesus, the Anointed One. Jesus demonstrates on Mount Hermon what Psalm 133 kind of unity looks like.

It looks a lot like me shutting up and listening to Jesus!

Returning to earth from this mountaintop experience with his three friends, the first job Jesus tackles is to evict (remember *ekballo*?) a demon from a young boy's life (Luke 9:37–40). This whole story is a powerful demonstration of the kingdom of heaven invading earth. As the Christed One releasing a poor boy from the tyranny of demonic influence, Jesus is swinging his battering ram into the very gates of Hades.

The invitation to come up the mountain with Jesus, to be hidden in him as we experience first-hand the glory of God, is open to each one of us. There is a unique place with your or my name on it, waiting for another human being to be ushered into the council chamber of God to act as a negotiator on behalf of individuals, or even nations. There are demonic squatters to be evicted, sick people to be healed, the poor to be given the good news. The Anointed One, the Christ, could do all of this himself, or send angels, but for some reason he loves to use little funny people like us. He loves to share his business, his power and his very nature with the likes of you and me.

Welcome to the Christing.

Notes

Preface

[1] As I began thinking and preaching about the Christing, I felt the need of a companion in my thinking process, then stumbled on Alexander MacLaren's *Bible Expositions*. The particular references of interest are *Expositions of Holy Scripture* (Amazon Kindle Edition), 2 Corinthians 1:21, Psalm 105:14–15.

1: Open Heaven

[1] Genesis 25:26 ESV Bible footnote: 'Jacob means, he takes by the heel, or he cheats.'

[2] John 3:3.

[3] Revelation 21:3.

[4] Psalm 132:15,16.

[5] 'For there is one God, and there is one mediator between God and men, the man Christ Jesus' (1 Timothy 2:5).

[6] Exodus 34:35.

[7] 'And without faith it is impossible to please God, because anyone who comes to him must believe that he exists and that he rewards those who earnestly seek him' Hebrews 11:6 (NIV).

8   'After this, the word of the LORD came to Abram in a vision: "Do not be afraid, Abram. I am your shield, your very great reward"' Genesis 15:1 (NIV).

9   'For you have died, and your life is hidden with Christ in God' (Colossians 3:3).

3: Manifesto

1   Luke 1:15.
2   Matthew 5:3.

4: Apart

1   1 Kings 10:7.
2   Isaiah lists names of the Messiah: 'Wonderful Counsellor, Mighty God, Everlasting Father, Prince of Peace' (Isaiah 9:6).
3   'But as it is, Christ has obtained a ministry that is as much more excellent than the old as the covenant he mediates is better, since it is enacted on better promises' (Hebrews 8:6).
4   Colossians 1:15–20.
5   Exodus 30:32.
6   Amy Collier Artman, *The Miracle Lady: Kathryn Kuhlman and the Transformation of Charismatic Christianity* (Grand Rapids, MI: Eerdmans, 2019).
7   The Aaronic Blessing: 'The LORD spoke to Moses, saying, "Speak to Aaron and his sons, saying, Thus you shall bless the people of Israel: you shall say to them, The LORD bless you and keep you; the LORD make his face to shine upon you and be gracious to you; the LORD lift up his countenance upon you and give you peace. So shall they put my name upon the people of Israel, and I will bless them"' (Numbers 6:22–27).
8   Matthew 9:1–7.

5: Executive Power

[1] J.H. Thayer, *Thayer's Greek Definitions* (Public Domain, 1896).
[2] Matthew 7:29.
[3] John 10:18.
[4] John Wimber with Kevin Springer, *Power Evangelism* (London UK: Hodder & Stoughton, 1985).
[5] Ed Silvoso, *Prayer Evangelism* (Grand Rapids, MI: Chosen Books, 2000).

6: Craftsmen and Governors

[1] See Daniel 3.
[2] 'As for these four youths, God gave them learning and skill in all literature and wisdom, and Daniel had understanding in all visions and dreams. At the end of the time, when the king had commanded that they should be brought in, the chief of the eunuchs brought them in before Nebuchadnezzar. And the king spoke with them, and among all of them none was found like Daniel, Hananiah, Mishael, and Azariah. Therefore they stood before the king. And in every matter of wisdom and understanding about which the king inquired of them, he found them ten times better than all the magicians and enchanters that were in all his kingdom' (Daniel 1:17–20).
[3] The book of Daniel is written partly in Hebrew and partly Aramaic. Critics have argued that the use of the Aramaic language indicates a much later time of writing. However, Aramaic was in use in international relations by the time of King Hezekiah (2 Kings 18). Daniel worked at the highest level in the court of Babylon, no doubt requiring fluent Babylonian, then served the Medo-Persian Empire under Darius the Mede.
[4] Genesis 42.

7: All Flesh

[1] Not all evangelicals believe in the Baptism of the Holy Spirit as a specific separate event to the New Birth, but most of those who do would insist that repenting and believing in Jesus must come before we can receive the Holy Spirit. A good book on the subject is: Randy Clark, *Baptized in the Spirit: God's Presence Resting Upon You with Power* (Shippensburg, PA: Destiny Image, 2017).

[2] The word translated 'spirit' in the Bible has a similar meaning in both languages, however in each case there are multiple layers of complementary ideas. The Hebrew is *ruwach*, meaning 'breath, wind, animation'; in Greek it is *pneuma*, meaning 'breath, wind, the spirit'. It can mean the spirit of a man or the Spirit of God. Jesus picks up the idea of the wind in John 3:8, and there is the sound of 'a mighty rushing wind' at Pentecost when the Spirit comes (Acts 2).

[3] Philippians 2:4.

[4] When Paul and Silas arrived at Thessalonica, within three weeks they had caused such a stir that they were being hunted by the authorities. It was there that it was said, 'These men who have turned the world upside down have come here also, and Jason has received them, and they are all acting against the decrees of Caesar, saying that there is another king, Jesus' (Acts 17:6–7).

8: Weak Superheroes

[1] Isaiah 9:6.

9: Properly Pickled

[1] James Strong, *Strong's Definitions* (Public Domain).

[2] J.H. Thayer, *Thayer's Greek Definitions* (Public Domain, 1896).

10: Sons of Fresh Oil

[1] John 8:12.

11: Oily Lovers

[1] God rebuked King Saul, through the prophet Samuel, 'But now your kingdom shall not continue. The LORD has sought out a man after his own heart, and the LORD has commanded him to be prince over his people, because you have not kept what the LORD commanded you' (1 Samuel 13:14).

[2] https://twitter.com/ChristineCaine 8.50 p.m. – 21 February 2018.

[3] Matthew 26:10.

[4] John 4:23,24.

[5] The church is sometimes referred to as the Bride of Christ (see Revelation 19:7). It's a powerful metaphor which describes the jealous love which God has for his people. It points to the level of intimacy between a human husband and wife in our relationship with him (see also Ephesians 5:21–33). In Revelation 21:2 she is described as the 'new Jerusalem'.

[6] Galatians 5:22.

[7] James Strong, *Strong's Definitions* (Public Domain). Strong's Number H1523.

[8] James Strong, *The New Strong's Exhaustive Concordance of the Bible* (Public Domain). Strong's Number G21 and G242.

[9] Acts 13:48.

12: More, Please?

[1] Matthew 25:14–30.

[2] Jesus said, 'But whoever drinks of the water that I will give him will never be thirsty again. The water that I will give him will

become in him a spring of water welling up to eternal life' (John 4:14). Or: 'Anyone who drinks this water will soon become thirsty again. But those who drink the water I give will never be thirsty again. It becomes a fresh, bubbling spring within them, giving them eternal life' (John 4:13–14 NLT). If we drink the water Jesus gives – the Holy Spirit – we then have a source inside us which nourishes us with life. We also become a source to those around us.

13: Flesh v. Spirit

[1] Hebrews 7:19.

[2] James Strong, *Strong's Definitions* (Public Domain). Strong's Number H5753: '*âvâh, aw-vaw*'; a primitive root; to crook, literally or figuratively: do amiss, bow down, make crooked, commit iniquity, pervert, (do) perverse(-ly), trouble, turn, do wickedly, do wrong.

[3] Caroline Leaf, *Who Switched Off My Brain?* (Southlake, TX: Inprov, 2009).

[4] Ezekiel 11:19.

[5] Sergius Bolshakoff, *The Russian Mystics* (Kalamazoo, MI: Cistercian Publications, 1980). Copyright 1976 by Cistercian Publications, Inc. © 2008 by Order of Saint Benedict, Collegeville, Minnesota. Used with permission.

[6] Hebrews 4:16; 1 John 4:18.

14: The Cloud

[1] Genesis 1:31.

15: Breaking Yokes

1   James Strong, *Strong's Definitions* (Public Domain). Strong's Number H8080: *shemen, sheh'-men*; from H8080; grease, especially liquid (as from the olive, often perfumed); figuratively, richness: anointing, fat (things), fruitful, oil(-ed), ointment, olive, pine.

2   'Therefore, if anyone is in Christ, he is a new creation. The old has passed away; behold the new has come. All this is from God, who through Christ reconciled us to himself and gave us the ministry of reconciliation; that is, in Christ God was reconciling the world to himself, not counting their trespasses against them, and entrusting to us the message of reconciliation. Therefore, we are ambassadors for Christ, God making his appeal through us' (2 Corinthians 5:17–20).

3   See note 1.

17: The Lord's Anointed

1   The Nazirite code of conduct: Numbers 6:1–21.

18: Anti Christ

1   Gerald B. Smith, ed., *The Tozer Pulpit* (WingSpread, 3rd edition, 1994).

2   A.W. Tozer, *The Counsellor* (WingSpread, 1993).

19: Raising Young Messiahs

1   Luke 1:48.

The Good God

Enjoying Father, Son, and Spirit

Michael Reeves

Why is God love? *Because God is a Trinity.*

Why can we be saved? *Because God is a Trinity.*

How are we able to live the Christian life? *Through the Trinity.*

In this lively and refreshing book, we find an accessible
introduction to the profound beauty of the Trinity. With wit and
clarity, Reeves draws from notable teachers from church history
to the present to reveal how the Christian life is rooted in the
triune God - Father, Son and Spirit. Be encouraged to grow in
enjoyment of God and see how God's triune being makes all his
ways beautiful.

978-1-84227-744-7

Christ Our Life

Celebrating the joy of knowing Jesus

Michael Reeves

How can we know who God is? *We look to Jesus.*
How can we live a godly life? *We look to Jesus.*
How do we know we can be saved? *We look to Jesus.*

In this lively and refreshing book, we find an accessible intro-duction to the profound glory and wonder of Christ. With wit and clarity, Michael Reeves, author of bestselling *The Good God*, draws from notable teachers from church history to the present to reveal a deeper and richer understanding of who Jesus is, his life on earth, his death and resurrection and his anticipated return. Rather than just merely adding to our knowledge about Jesus, this book is a call to consider Christ more deeply so that he might become more central for you, that you might know him better, treasure him more, and enter into his joy.

Be encouraged to look upon Jesus and see how he is indeed our life, our righteousness, our holiness and our hope.

978-1-84227-758-4

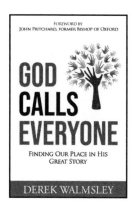

God Calls Everyone

*Finding our place in
his great story*

Derek Walmsley

What are we supposed to do with our lives? Does God have a plan
for us?

If you have ever asked these questions, then this book will help
you to discern what your vocation might be. Through the lens of
the Bible's whole narrative, you are invited to take part in God's
story, and what he is doing, rather than asking what we can do for
God. Questions at the end of each chapter allow you to reflect on
the characteristics and attitudes needed for serving God.

Whether you are considering full-time ministry or wondering
where you fit into God's plan, this is an accessible and engaging
look at the joyous celebration of God calling us all to be part of
his story.

978-1-78893-108-3

The Man in White

Extraordinary accounts of the intervening power of the living God

Dr Ernest F. Crocker

Many of us want to see Jesus, to hear his voice. We want a tangible experience of God.

As a Christian doctor and follower of Jesus, Ernest Crocker has been a witness to many interventions of God during his life. In *The Man in White*, he brings together an inspiring selection of testimonies from around the world of people who have seen God do extraordinary things in and through their lives. They include professionals, academics, a train robber, a surgeon facing decapitation for his faith, and those who have escaped the ravages of war.

These powerful stories inspire and challenge us to see that God is real and delights in being involved in our lives today.

978-1-78893-133-5

Blood, Sweat and Jesus

The story of a Christian hospital bringing hope and healing in a Muslim community

Kerry Stillman

What is a Christian hospital doing in a remote Muslim area of Cameroon?

Kerry Stillman shares her own experiences of working as a physiotherapist in a sub-Saharan village hospital. A vivid impression of daily life is painted as the team deal with the threat of terrorism, the attitudes of local people towards Western medicine, their patients' health issues, and the challenge of sensitively sharing the gospel in a different culture.

Passionate, intriguing and uplifting, this is a colourful interweaving of cultures, beliefs and the power of prayer alongside modern medicine.

978-1-78893-148-9

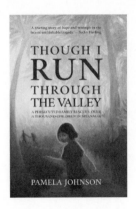

Though I Run Through the Valley

A persecuted family rescues over a thousand children in Myanmar

Pamela Johnson

Amid decades of war and political strife in Myanmar one family fights back with their weapon of choice - the Bible.

Three generations of Emmeline's family have been living out their love for God by rescuing children who have been orphaned, abandoned or made destitute by their country's upheaval. Theirs is not a story of merely evading the enemy and surviving, but instead one of seeking out the vulnerable and teaching them how to thrive.

Daring to trust God against all the odds, this is the powerful story of one family's sacrifice to provide a home for orphans so that the children of Myanmar could hope for a better future.

978-1-78893-160-1

A Beautiful Tapestry

*Two ordinary women,
one amazing God,
many lives transformed*

*Tracy Williamson
with Marilyn Baker*

Being blind, Marilyn's childhood was one of increasing isolation whilst Tracy's was marked by deafness and low self-esteem. Yet from these most unlikely of origins, God brought these two remarkable ladies together in the most hilarious fashion and gave them a joint vision to work together through Marilyn Baker Ministries.

Through their work in prisons, concerts, retreats, conferences and prayer ministry, they have seen many lives transformed by the power of God's love. Many of those testimonies are included in this book, showing that God is indeed weaving a beautiful tapestry in all our lives. Each individual strand of yarn isn't much in itself, but when woven together an amazing picture emerges as he uses us in our weakness to show the beauty of his love to others.

978-1-78893-156-4

Ever Present

*Running to survive, thrive
and believe*

Austen Hardwick

Strokes, brain surgery, epilepsy . . . where is God in the middle of
our suffering?

After surviving three strokes in his forties, Austen Hardwick
began to think more deeply about life and faith. As he started to
recover, he realised that running created space in which he could
draw closer to God.

Weaving together personal testimony and biblical teaching,
Austen encourages us to run towards God rather than away from
him, so that we, too, can learn to live life in all its fullness with an
ever-present God who is with us in our struggles.

Genuine, real, and inspirational, *Ever Present* explores how
running can be good for both the heart and the soul.

978-1-78893-136-6

Salt Water and Honey

*Lost dreams, good grief,
and a better story*

Lizzie Lowrie

Reeling from the disappointment of a failed business venture, Lizzie Lowrie's life takes a nightmarish turn as she suffers miscarriage after miscarriage.

Written from the messy middle of life, where there are no neat or cliched answers, Lizzie honestly shares her pain and the fight to find God in her suffering.

Providing a safe space to remind people that they're not alone, it's okay to grieve and their story matters, this is for anyone who has lost their dream and is struggling to understand their purpose when life looks nothing like they hoped it would.

978-1-78893-095-6

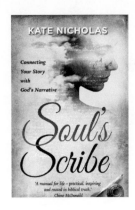

Soul's Scribe

Connecting your story with God's narrative

Kate Nicholas

Each of us has a soul story to tell – the unique story of how we experience God throughout our lives.

Kate Nicholas expertly takes you on a journey through the various stages of your life, helping you to see your soul's story as an adventure full of meaning and purpose, connecting your tale with the great sweeping arc of God's eternal narrative.

As you identify the main themes of your life that connect past and present, you will be able to understand your life as a coherent whole. And at the end of this reflective and practical process, you will have the tools to step out and tell your own story with confidence.

Point others to Jesus as you are empowered to share the good things God has done for you.

978-1-78893-021-5

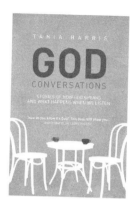

God Conversations

*Stories of how God speaks and
what happens when we listen*

Tania Harris

Stories of God talking to his people abound throughout the
Bible, but we usually only get the highlights. We read: 'God
said "Go to Egypt,"' and then, 'Mary and Joseph left for
Egypt.' We're not told how God spoke, how they knew it was
him, or how they decided to act on what they'd heard.

In *God Conversations*, international speaker and pastor Tania
Harris shares insights from her own story of learning to hear
God's voice. You'll get to eavesdrop on some contemporary
conversations with God in the light of his communication
with the ancients. Part memoir, part teaching, this unique and
creative collection will help you to recognize God's voice when
he speaks and what happens when you do.

978-1-78078-188-4

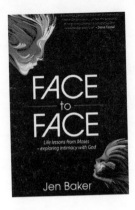

Face to Face

*Life lessons from Moses –
exploring intimacy with God*

Jen Baker

God longs for us to personally experience more of him, but so often we refuse or feel unable to draw close to him. Even the great hero of faith Moses hid his face from God, yet was eventually transformed into someone who spoke face to face with him.

Jen Baker explores Moses' life to see how he was able to move from hiddenness to holiness and encourages us to follow his example. Interwoven with personal testimony, Jen gently challenges and shows us how to move out of the shadows into the light of God's love.

Whether you feel distant from God or want to deepen your relationship with him, *Face to Face* will help encourage you to experience God in a new and powerful way.

978-1-78893-056-7

Our Precious Lives

*Why telling and hearing stories
can save the church*

Steve Morris

In a world of increasing social fragmentation and loneliness,
Our Precious Lives demonstrates how listening to others can be
transformational in creating a sense of belonging. Inspiring stories
are grounded by practical ideas to put storytelling at the heart
of the church, and questions in each chapter encourage us all to
glimpse more of God, revel in our uniqueness and realize that we
all have something valuable to offer as his followers.

Underpinned by practical pastoral experience, this is a book full
of quirky and unexpected life stories that open us up afresh to the
beauty of life and our God.

978-1-78893-079-6

Authentic

We trust you enjoyed reading this book from Authentic. If you want to be informed of any new titles from this author and other releases you can sign up to the Authentic newsletter by scanning below:

Online:
authenticmedia.co.uk

Follow us: